Janice VanCleave's

Energy
for Every Kid

Other Titles by Janice VanCleave

Science for Every Kid series:
Janice VanCleave's Astronomy for Every Kid
Janice VanCleave's Biology for Every Kid
Janice VanCleave's Chemistry for Every Kid
Janice VanCleave's Constellations for Every Kid
Janice VanCleave's Dinosaurs for Every Kid
Janice VanCleave's Earth Science for Every Kid
Janice VanCleave's Ecology for Every Kid
Janice VanCleave's Food and Nutrition for Every Kid
Janice VanCleave's Geography for Every Kid
Janice VanCleave's Geometry for Every Kid
Janice VanCleave's The Human Body for Every Kid
Janice VanCleave's Math for Every Kid
Janice VanCleave's Oceans for Every Kid
Janice VanCleave's Physics for Every Kid

Spectacular Science Projects series:
Janice VanCleave's Animals
Janice VanCleave's Earthquakes
Janice VanCleave's Electricity
Janice VanCleave's Gravity
Janice VanCleave's Insects and Spiders
Janice VanCleave's Machines
Janice VanCleave's Magnets
Janice VanCleave's Microscopes and Magnifying Lenses
Janice VanCleave's Molecules
Janice VanCleave's Plants
Janice VanCleave's Rocks and Minerals
Janice VanCleave's Solar System
Janice VanCleave's Volcanoes
Janice VanCleave's Weather

Also:
Janice VanCleave's 200 Gooey, Slippery, Slimy, Weird, and Fun Experiments
Janice VanCleave's 201 Awesome, Magical, Bizarre, and Incredible Experiments
Janice VanCleave's 202 Oozing, Bubbling, Dripping, and Bouncing Experiments
Janice VanCleave's 203 Icy, Freezing, Frosty, and Cool Experiments
Janice VanCleave's 204 Sticky, Gloppy, Wacky, and Wonderful Experiments
Janice VanCleave's Guide to the Best Science Fair Projects
Janice VanCleave's Guide to More of the Best Science Fair Projects
Janice VanCleave's Science Around the Year
Janice VanCleave's Science Through the Ages
Janice VanCleave's Scientists
Janice VanCleave's Science Around the World

Janice VanCleave's

Energy
for Every Kid

WILEY

John Wiley & Sons, Inc.

This book is printed on acid-free paper. ∞

Published by John Wiley & Sons, Inc., Hoboken, New Jersey
Published simultaneously in Canada

For general information about our other products and services, please contact our Customer Care Department within the United States at (800) 762-2974, outside the United States at (317) 572-3993 or fax (317) 572-4002.

Wiley also publishes its books in a variety of electronic formats. Some content that appears in print may not be available in electronic books. For more information about Wiley products, visit our web site at www.wiley.com.

Library of Congress Cataloging-in-Publication Data:

VanCleave, Janice Pratt.
  [Energy for every kid]
  Janice VanCleave's energy for every kid / Janice VanCleave.
      p. cm.—(Science for every kid series)
  Includes index.
  ISBN-13 978-0-471-33099-8 (paper: alk. paper)
  ISBN-10 0-471-33099-X (paper: alk. paper)
  1. Force and energy—Juvenile literature. 2. Power resources—Juvenile literature.
I. Title: Energy for every kid. II. Title.
  QC73.4.V36 2005
  531'.6—dc22

                                                                          2004027114

Printed in the United States of America

10 9 8 7 6 5 4 3 2 1

It is with pleasure that I dedicate this book to a special group of young scientists who are members of Sonoran Desert Homeschoolers. The motto of this group is *hozho* (Navajo for "walking in beauty and friendship"). This group field-tested the activities in this book and their input was invaluable in making the book easy and fun:

Karen, Bean, and Cate Metcalf and Kyla Ballard

Acknowledgments

A special note of gratitude goes to these educators who assisted by pretesting the activities and/or by providing scientific information: I wish to express my appreciation to James H. Hunderfund, Ed.D., Superintendent of Schools; Pamela J. Travis-Moore, Principal; and James Engeldrum, Science Chairperson. Because of the approval and the support of these supervisors, the following students at Commack Middle School, under the direction of Diane M. Flynn and Ellen M. Vlachos, tested and/or provided ideas for activities in this book: Danny Abrams, Louis Arens, Scott Aronin, Jesse Badash, Rachel Bloom, Randi Bloom, Ryan William Brown, Christopher Caccamo, Tia Canonico, Jenna Cecchini, Jennifer Ciampi, Melissa Coates, Sarah Corey, Vincent Daigger, Alana Davicino, John Halloran, Saba Javadi, Jamie Keller, Kevin Kim, Matthew J. Kim, Joshua Krongelb, Arielle Lewen, Alexandra Lionetti, Taylor Macy, Taylor Manoussos, Ian Ross Marquit, David Murphy, Bryan D. Noonan, Stephanie Pennetti, Erica Portnoy, GemmaRose Ragozzine, Arpon Raksit, Ayden Rosenberg, Danielle Simone, Daniel E. Scholem, Hunter Smith, Allison Smithwick, Evan Sunshine, Marni Wasserman, Daniel Weissman, Chris Wenz, Christopher M. Zambito, Ashlyn Wiebalck, Aaron Wilson, and Alice Zhou. I also want to thank the following children for their help and ideas: Rachel, Jared, and Sara Cathey, and Weston and Easton Walker.

Contents

     Direct Heating by Solar Energy

25   Pass It On   185
     Energy Transfers within a Community

     Glossary   197
     Index   215

Introduction

This is a basic book about energy that is designed to teach facts, concepts, and problem-solving strategies. Each section introduces concepts about energy in a way that makes learning useful and fun.

Energy is the ability to do work. **Work** is done when a **force** (a push or pull on an object) causes an object to move. Thus, energy is the capacity to make things change, and the process of making them change is called work. In this book, unless otherwise stated, it is assumed that there is no energy loss and the total amount of energy transferred to an object is changed to work. There are different kinds of energy, including sound, heat, electricity, and light.

This book will not provide all the answers about energy, but it will guide you in discovering answers to questions relating to energy such as, Why do some logs in a fireplace have multicolored flames? When strummed, why do different strings on a guitar have different sounds? When stirring something hot, why can you feel the heat when you use a spoon with a metal handle but not when you use one with a wooden handle? Why does hot chocolate in a Styrofoam cup stay warmer than if it were in a paper cup?

This book presents energy information in a way that you can easily understand and use. It is designed to teach energy concepts so that they can be applied to many similar situations. The exercises, experiments, and other activities were selected for their ability to explain concepts in basic terms with little complexity. One of the main objectives of the book is to present the *fun* of learning about energy.

How to Use This Book

Read each chapter slowly and follow procedures carefully. You will learn best if each section is read in order, as there is some buildup of information as the book progresses. The format for each chapter is as follows:

- **What You Need to Know:** Background information and an explanation of terms.

- **Exercises:** Questions to be answered or situations to be solved using the information from What You Need to Know.

- **Activity:** A project to allow you to apply the skill to a problem-solving situation in the real world.

- **Solutions to Exercises:** Step-by-step instructions for solving the Exercises.

All **boldfaced** terms are defined in a Glossary at the end of the book. Be sure to flip back to the Glossary as often as you need to, making each term part of your personal vocabulary.

General Instructions for the Exercises

1. Study each problem carefully by reading it through once or twice before answering.

2. Check your answers in the Solutions to Exercises to evaluate your work.

3. Do the work again if any of your answers are incorrect.

General Instructions for the Activities

1. Read each activity completely before starting.

2. Collect needed supplies. You will have less frustration and more fun if all the necessary materials for the activi-

ties are ready before you start. You lose your train of thought when you have to stop and search for supplies.

3. Do not rush through the activity. Follow each step very carefully; never skip steps, and do not add your own. Safety is of utmost importance, and by reading each activity before starting, then following the instructions exactly, you can feel confident that no unexpected results will occur.

4. Observe. If your results are not the same as described in the activity, carefully reread the instructions and start over from step 1.

1
Moving Stuff
Energy and Work

What You Need to Know

Energy is the capacity to make things change, and the process of making them change is called work. **Work** (*w*) is accomplished when a **force** (*f*) (a push or a pull on an object) causes an object to move, which is also the process of transferring energy. Thus, **energy** is the ability to do work.

The amount of work can be determined by multiplying the force by the distance (*d*) along which the force is applied. The equation for work is:

work = force × distance

$$w = f \times d$$

In the English system of measuring, a **pound** is a unit of force and a **foot** is a unit of distance. Therefore, the common unit for work in the English system of measuring is **foot-pounds (ft-lb)**. In the metric system, **newton (N)** is a force unit and **meter (m)** is a distance unit. The newton-meter work unit in the metric system is called a **joule (J)**. One joule is about 0.74 ft-lb.

Since energy and work are related, without any loss of energy, a given amount of energy can do an equal amount of work. So the work done in lifting an object is equal to the energy given to the object. If you want to lift an object, you must apply a force equal to the weight of the object. For example, to lift a 10-pound (45-N) dog onto a table that is 3 feet (0.9 m) high, you must apply a force equal to the weight of the dog as you raise the dog 3 feet (0.9 m). The work done in lifting the dog is:

English Measurements	**Metric Measurements**
$w = f \times d$	$w = 45 \text{ N} \times 0.9 \text{ m}$
$= 10 \text{ lb} \times 3 \text{ ft}$	$= 40.5 \text{ Nm}$
$= 30 \text{ ft-lb}$	$= 40.5 \text{ J}$

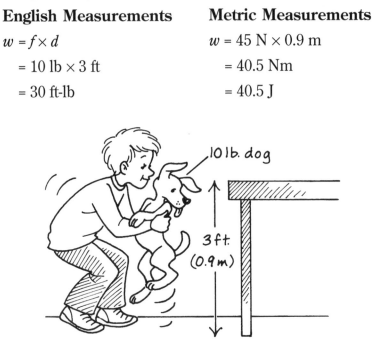

The work done in lifting the dog is 30 foot-pounds, which is the same as 40.5 joules of **kinetic energy (KE)** (the energy of moving objects). The energy of objects lifted above a surface is called **potential energy** (stored energy of an object due to its position or condition). Thus, while sitting on the table, the dog has 30 foot-pounds (40.5 J) of energy more than he had when sitting on the floor.

Let's suppose that instead of lifting the dog, you put the dog on a blanket and slide the blanket 3 feet (0.9 m) across the floor. The weight of the dog doesn't change, but you do not have to use as much force in pulling the dog to move him 3 feet (0.9 m) as you did in lifting him 3 feet (0.9 m). This is because to lift the dog, you have to overcome the pull of **gravity** (the force of attraction that exists between any two objects). Earth's gravity pulls objects near or on Earth toward Earth's center.

Weight is a measure of the force of gravity on an object. When the dog is sitting on the floor, the dog's weight is the force pushing the blanket and the floor together. To move the dog across the floor, you have to overcome the friction between the blanket and the floor. **Friction** is the force that opposes the motion of objects whose surfaces are in contact with each other. The amount of friction between two surfaces depends on the force pushing the surfaces together and the roughness of the surfaces. Since the floor is horizontal, the weight of the dog is equal to the force pushing the blanket and the floor together. If the blanket and floor are slick, the frictional force is less than the weight of the dog. So the force needed to drag the dog across the floor might be only 2.5 pounds (11.25 N). Thus, the work done in moving the dog across the slick floor would be:

$w = f \times d$

$\quad = 2.5 \text{ lb } (11.25 \text{ N}) \times 3 \text{ ft } (0.9 \text{ m})$

$\quad = 7.5 \text{ ft-lb } (10.13 \text{ J})$

As before, the work done on the dog is equal to the energy given to the dog. But since the dog is not lifted, the energy given to the dog is not potential energy. Instead, it is kinetic energy. See chapters 3, 4, and 5 for more information about potential and kinetic energy.

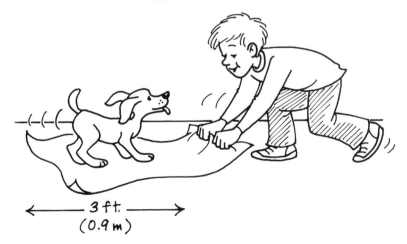

$\longleftarrow$ 3 ft. $\longrightarrow$
(0.9 m)

Exercises

1. How many foot-pounds of work would be done in lifting barbells weighing 200 pounds to a height of 5 feet?

2. How many joules of work are done if it takes 45 N of force to drag a sled 10 m uphill?

Activity: UPHILL

Purpose   To compare the work done in moving an object by different methods.

Materials   scissors
rubber band
paper clip
paper hole punch
4-by-10-inch (10-by-25-cm) piece of corrugated
   cardboard
metric ruler
pen
4 tablespoons (60 ml) dirt (sand or salt will
   work)
empty soda can with metal tab
24-inch (60-cm) piece of string
4 or more books

Procedure

1. Cut the rubber band to form one long piece.

2. Tie one end of the rubber band to the paper clip. Open one end of the paper clip to form a hook.

3. Using the paper hole punch, cut a hole in the center of the edge of the cardboard.

4. Tie the free end of the rubber band in the hole in the cardboard. The top of the paper clip should reach the center of the cardboard.

5. Use the ruler and pen to draw a line across the cardboard, making it even with the top of the paper clip. Label the line 0.

6. Then draw as many lines as possible 1 cm apart below the 0 line. You have made a scale.

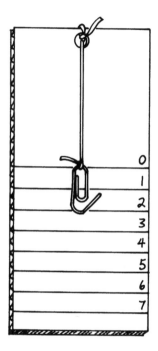

7. Pour the dirt into the soda can.

8. Thread the string through the hole in the tab of the soda can. Tie the ends of the string together to make a loop.

9. Place the string loop over the hook on the scale.

10. Stack all of the books except one. Lean the extra book against the stacked books to form a ramp as shown.

11. Stand the can next to the stack of books. Then lift the can straight up by pulling on the top of the cardboard until the bottom of the can is even with the top of the books. Note the scale line closest to the top of the paper clip hook.

12. Lay the can on the book ramp. With the scale still attached to the string, drag the can to the top of the ramp. Again note the scale line closest to the top of the paper clip hook as the can is being moved.

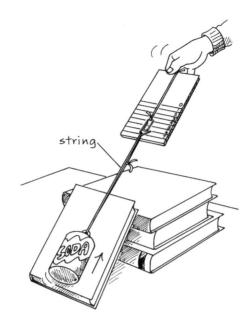

string

Results The rubber band stretches more when the can is lifted straight up than when it is pulled up the ramp. So the number on the scale when you pulled the can straight up was higher than the number when you were pulling the can up the ramp.

Why? Gravity pulls the can down. When you lift the can straight up, the rubber band scale indicates the full pull of gravity, which is the weight of the can. The work done in lifting the can to the height of the stacked books is the product of the weight of the can times the height of the books.

A **ramp** is a tilted surface used to move objects to a higher level. A ramp is called a **machine** because it is a device that helps you do work. When using a machine, you generally have to use less effort. For example, the decrease in the amount the can on the ramp stretched the rubber band indicates that the force needed to pull the can up the ramp is less than that needed to lift the can straight up. It takes less effort to drag the can up the ramp, but the can moved a longer distance. While it takes less effort to move an object up a ramp, the overall work done is more than the work in lifting the can because of friction between the can and the ramp. The effort force in moving the can up the ramp depends on the friction between the can and the ramp. A smooth ramp would require less effort than a rough one.

Solutions to Exercises

1. *Think!*

- Work is the product of force needed to move an object times the distance the object moves. The equation is $w = f \times d$.

- Foot-pounds (ft-lb) is the English unit for work if the force is measured in pounds and the distance in feet.

- The force needed to lift an object is equal to its weight. So the work done in lifting the barbells is $w = 200 \text{ lb} \times 5 \text{ ft}$.

The work done in lifting the barbells is 1,000 ft-lb.

2. *Think!*

- Joules (J) is the metric unit of work if the force is measured in newtons (N) and the distance in meters (m).

- $w = f \times d$

- $w = 45 \text{ N} \times 10 \text{ m}$

The work done in moving the sled is 450 J.

2

Constant

The Law of Conservation of Mass and Energy

What You Need to Know

The **universe** (Earth and all natural objects in space regarded as a whole) is made of matter. **Matter** is anything that takes up space and has **mass** (amount of material in a substance). A **gram (g)** is a metric unit for measuring mass. On Earth matter exists in three basic forms, or states: solid, liquid, and gas. The weights of objects can be used to compare their masses. The greater the weight, the greater the mass.

Atoms are the building blocks of matter. Basic chemical substances composed of only one kind of an atom are called **elements**. Atoms are held together by a force called a **bond**. Substances made of two or more different atoms linked together by bonds are called **compounds**. There are two types of compounds: ionic compounds and molecular compounds. **Ionic compounds**, such as sodium chloride (table salt), are made of stacks of **ions** (an atom or a group of atoms with an electrical charge). **Molecular compounds**, such as water, are made of molecules. A **molecule** is the smallest physical unit of a molecular compound.

In the eighteenth century, the French chemist Antoine Lavoisier (1743–1794) was the first to recognize that during a **chemical reaction** (the process in which atoms in substances rearrange to form new substances) matter cannot be created or destroyed. In other words, all the atoms making up the chemicals of the **reactants** (the starting materials in a chemical reaction) are rearranged so that they form the **products** (the materials produced in a chemical reaction).

Because the total amount of mass in a chemical reaction is **conserved** (remains constant) the mass of the reactants equals the mass of the products. This relationship is called the **law of conservation of mass**. Chemicals contain **chemical energy**, which is the energy in the bonds that hold atoms together. Chemical energy is a form of potential energy called **chemical potential energy**. This energy is released when the bonds between atoms are broken during a chemical reaction.

In the nineteenth century, what is now called the **law of conservation of energy** was first described by the German scientist Julius Robert von Mayer (1814–1878). This law states that under ordinary conditions energy can change from one form to another, but the sum total of all the energy in the universe remains constant. In other words, like matter, energy can neither be created nor destroyed but can only be **transformed** (changed from one form into another). For example, if you push a box across a floor, the energy that comes from the food you eat is transferred to the box.

Atoms are made up of the **nucleus** (the center of an atom), which contains **protons** (positively charged particles) and **neutrons** (particles with no charge), and **electrons** (negatively charged particles), which are found outside the nucleus. In 1905, Albert Einstein determined that during certain extraordinary conditions mass can be changed into energy and energy into mass. These special conditions are called **nuclear reactions** (changes in the nuclei of atoms). To include extraordinary conditions, the separate laws of conservation of matter and of energy can be combined into the **law of conservation of mass and energy**. This law states that although matter and energy are interchangeable, they are not created or destroyed. Thus, the sum of all mass and energy in the universe is constant. A decrease in one causes an increase in the other.

In your everyday life, the separate laws of conservation of mass and energy under ordinary conditions apply. Thus, when speaking of a loss or gain of energy, it is understood to mean a transformation of one energy form to another. But when speaking specifically about nuclear changes, such as the breaking apart of a nucleus, there is a transformation from matter to energy or vice versa. See chapter 21 for information on nuclear changes.

Exercises

Use figures A and B to answer the following questions:

1. Which figure, A or B, represents the law of conservation of mass?

2. Which figure, A or B, is a nuclear change representing the law of conservation of mass and energy?

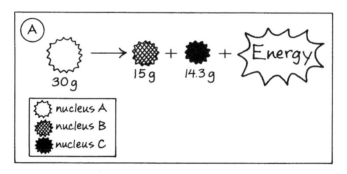

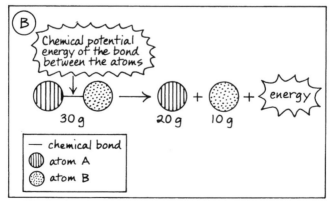

Activity: EQUAL

Purpose   To demonstrate conservation of mass during a chemical reaction.

Materials   two 3-ounce (90-ml) paper cups
measuring spoons
tap water
1 tablespoon (5 ml) Epsom salts
spoon
liquid school glue
food scale
paper towel

Procedure

1. In one of the paper cups, add 2 tablespoons (10 ml) of water and the Epsom salts. Stir the mixture until very little or no Epsom salts are left at the bottom of the cup.

2. Pour 1 tablespoon (5 ml) of liquid school glue into the second cup.

3. Set both cups on the scale. Note the appearance of the contents of each cup and their combined weight.

4. Pour the Epsom salts and water mixture into the cup of glue. Stir the contents of the cup. Note the appearance of the mixture in the cup.

5. With both the empty cup and the cup with the mixture on the scale, again note their combined weight and compare it to the combined weight of the cups before mixing their contents.

6. Once the weights have been compared, scoop out the white solid blob that has formed in the cup and place it on the paper towel. Fold the towel around the blob and squeeze the towel to press the extra liquid out of the blob. How does the blob differ from the reactants from which it was formed?

Results Originally, one cup contains a clear liquid made of Epsom salts and water, and the other contains white liquid glue. After mixing, a white solid blob of material is formed with some of the liquid left. The weights of the cups and their contents are the same before and after mixing.

Why? The mixture of Epsom salts and water forms a **solution** (a mixture of a substance that has been dissolved in a liquid). The liquid glue is also a solution containing different substances dissolved in water. When these two solutions are combined, a chemical reaction occurs between the materials as indicated by the formation of a white solid material. Even though the reactants break apart and recombine in different ways, all the original parts are contained inside the cup. Thus, when you weigh the cups the second time, there is no change in weight, which indicates there is no change in mass. So the conservation of mass during a chemical reaction is demonstrated.

Solutions to Exercises

1. *Think!*

- The law of conservation of mass states that matter is not created or destroyed during a chemical reaction.

- During a chemical reaction, the mass of the reactants equals the mass of the products.
- Which figure represents a chemical reaction and is therefore a representation of the law of conservation of mass?
- In the diagram, the bond between the atoms is broken. Thus, the released energy comes from the chemical potential energy stored in the bond.

Figure B represents the law of conservation of mass.

2. *Think!*

- The law of conservation of mass and energy states that during a nuclear reaction, the sum of mass and energy is constant.
- During a nuclear reaction, the original mass of the reactants may be more than the mass of the products. The lost mass is changed to an enormous amount of energy.
- Which figure represents a nuclear reaction in which there is a loss of mass and a great amount of energy produced, and is therefore a representation of the law of conservation of mass and energy?

Figure A represents the law of conservation of mass and energy.

3

Basic

Kinetic and Potential Energy

What You Need to Know

Objects have two basic kinds of energy: one is the energy of position and condition, also called stored energy or potential energy (PE), and the other is the energy of motion, which is known as kinetic energy (KE).

An object can have potential energy due to its position within a **force field**, which is a region that exerts a force of **attraction** (pulling together) or **repulsion** (pushing apart) on the object. For example, the **gravitational force field** around Earth is a region that attracts objects toward Earth. Potential energy increases when objects attracted to each other are pulled apart. For example, the **gravitational potential energy (GPE)** of a book increases by lifting it above the ground against the attractive force of gravity. Potential energy increases when objects that feel a repelling force are pushed together, such as when you compress a spring.

Kinetic energy is the energy that an object possesses because of its motion. Examples of objects with kinetic energy are moving cars, falling leaves, and particles in an object that move because the object is heated.

Energy is not created or destroyed, as stated in the law of conservation of energy; instead, it is transferred from one form to another. For example, if you are standing on a high-dive platform, you have gained potential energy by the work done in climbing the ladder against the force of gravity to the platform. Standing on the platform, you have maximum potential energy due to your position, and you have zero kinetic energy because you are not moving. When you dive off the platform, the potential energy changes into kinetic energy. As you get closer to the ground, your potential energy decreases and your kinetic energy increases. As you fall, you gain speed, and your kinetic energy increases.

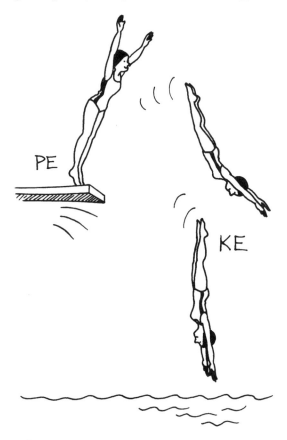

Exercises

1. Study the figure and determine the following:

   a. Which position, A, B, or C, represents the sled with the greatest potential energy?

   b. Which position, A, B, or C, represents the sled with the greatest kinetic energy?

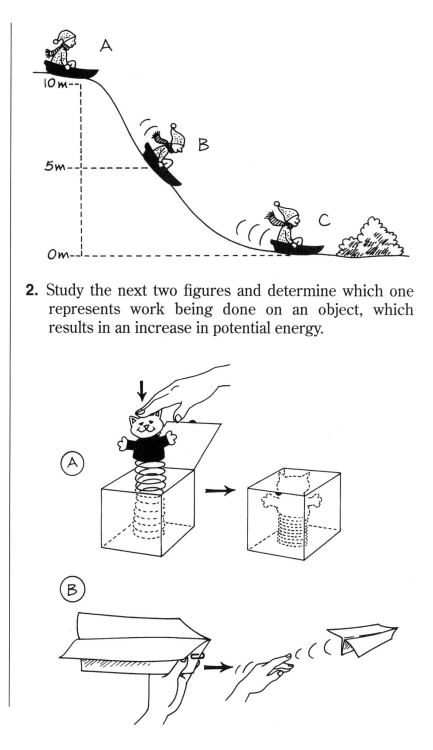

2. Study the next two figures and determine which one represents work being done on an object, which results in an increase in potential energy.

Activity: HOPPER

Purpose To demonstrate the relationship between kinetic and potential energy.

Materials 8-by-8-inch (20-by-20-cm) sheet of paper (use green paper if available)

        ruler

        pencil

Procedure

1. Fold the paper in half from side to side twice.

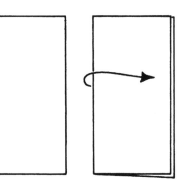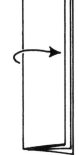

2. Unfold one of the folds.
3. Fold the top corners A and B over as shown.

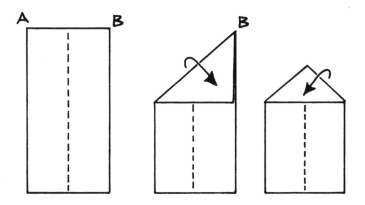

4. Unfold the corners. Use the ruler and pencil to draw lines C and D across the paper.

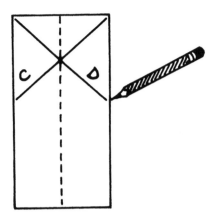

5. Fold the paper along line C. Then unfold the paper. Repeat folding and unfolding along line D.

6. Push in the sides of the top of the paper along the folded lines. Press the top down to form a triangle.

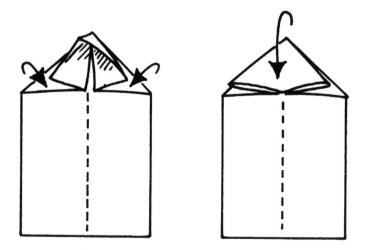

7. Fold the bottom of the paper over to meet the edge of the triangle at the top.

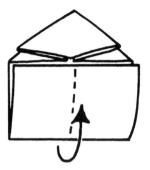

8. Bend one of the triangle points along the fold line. Then fold the side of the paper over to meet the center fold line.

9. Repeat step 8 with the other triangle point.

10. Fold the bottom edge over. Then fold part of it down as shown. You have made a leaping frog.

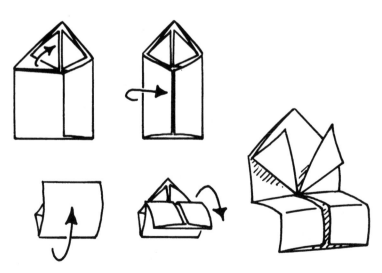

11. Use the pencil to draw eyes on the frog.

12. Stand the frog on a table and push down on its back with your finger so that the frog's back legs are compressed. Then quickly run your finger down the frog's back and off the end.

Results The frog will leap forward and possibly turn a somersault.

Why? When you press down on the frog, you are doing work on the frog, causing its folded legs to compress together much like a spring would be compressed. In this condition, the frog has potential energy. When you run your finger down the frog's back and off the folded end, this end is more compressed and the frog's head is raised. When you release the frog, the potential energy is transferred to kinetic energy as the frog leaps forward.

Solutions to Exercises

1a. *Think!*

* Objects at a height have potential energy, also called gravitational potential energy.

- The higher the object above a reference point (the bottom of the hill), the greater the potential energy. The sled is highest at position A in the example.

Position A represents the sled with the greatest potential energy.

b. *Think!*

- Moving objects have kinetic energy.
- The sled is moving at positions B and C.
- At position B, the sled is partway down the hill, so part of the sled's potential energy has been changed to kinetic energy.
- At position C, the sled is at the bottom of the hill, so the sled has zero potential energy and maximum kinetic energy.

Position C represents the sled with the greatest kinetic energy.

2. *Think!*

- Work is done when force on an object causes the object to move.
- As the jack-in-the-box in figure A is being pushed into the box, the spring on the toy is being compressed. Compressed springs have potential energy.
- In figure B, the paper airplane is being thrown. Objects that move have kinetic energy.

Figure A represents work being done on an object, which results in an increase in potential energy.

4

Stored

Potential Energy

What You Need to Know

Potential energy is the stored energy of an object due to its position or condition. The amount of work done on an object is equal to the amount of energy transferred to that object. If this energy is stored, then the object is given potential energy. This stored energy has the ability to do work when released. For example, a stretched rubber band acquires potential energy when work is done on it by the person who stretched it. The stretched rubber band is not moving; it has no kinetic energy, but it does have the potential of movement. If the band is part of a slingshot and it is released, the stretched band returns to its natural unstretched condition, and its potential energy is changed into kinetic energy. This energy is transferred to the pebble in the slingshot, which then has kinetic energy and moves forward. The stretched rubber band has **elastic potential energy**, which is the energy of materials that are in a state of being stretched or twisted.

Another form of potential energy is gravitational potential energy (GPE), which depends on the position of an object within Earth's gravitational field. The height and weight of an object affect its gravitational potential energy. This potential energy of an object increases as its height above a reference point increases. For example, the gravitational potential energy of a bucket of bricks raised above the ground is equal to the work done in lifting the bricks. Work is the product of the force needed to lift the bucket of bricks times the height they are lifted. This force is equal to the weight of the bucket of bricks. The relationship between gravitational potential energy, weight, which is the force due to gravity (f_{wt}), and height (h) can be expressed by the equation:

$$\text{GPE} = f_{wt} \times h$$

As more bricks are added to the raised bucket, the weight of the bucket increases, and the GPE of the raised bucket increases. So if a bucket with many bricks falls, it will do more work on the ground (meaning the ground receives energy when the bucket hits it) than a bucket with only a few bricks. The higher the object is above a surface, the greater the GPE of the object in reference to that surface. So a

bucket that falls from a higher height will do more work on the ground than a bucket of the same weight falling from a lower height. Note that the work done when the bucket hits the ground is equal to the gravitational potential energy of the bucket at its highest point above the ground if friction of the bucket with the air is not considered. **Air** is the mixture of gases making up Earth's **atmosphere** (the blanket of air surrounding Earth).

Chemical energy is a form of potential energy, also called chemical potential energy. This energy exists in the bonds (forces) that hold atoms together. When these bonds are broken, chemical energy changes into other energy forms, such as heat. For example, when fuel is burned or food is eaten, the bonds between atoms in these materials are broken and chemical energy changes into other energy forms. Two forms of potential energy due to attractive or repulsive forces between objects are nuclear and magnetic. The nucleus (the center of an atom) is where energy called **nuclear potential energy** is stored. This energy is due to forces between particles in the nucleus. When an atom's nucleus splits, a large amount of nuclear energy is released. Some objects near a magnet have **magnetic potential energy**, due to their attraction or repulsion to the magnet. (For more information on magnetic and nuclear potential energy see chapters 19 and 21.)

Exercises

1. A 40-pound (180 N) object is 6 feet (1.8 m) above the ground.

   a. What is the gravitational potential energy of the object?

   b. If friction is not considered, how much work can it do on the ground when the object falls?

2. Which figure, A, B, or C, represents the following:

   a. chemical potential energy

   b. gravitational potential energy

3. A stretched rubber band represents what type of potential energy?

Activity: HIGHER

Purpose   To determine the effect that height has on the gravitational potential energy of an object.

Materials   2 cups (500 ml) dry rice
                sock
                bathroom scale

Procedure

1. Pour the rice in the sock and tie a knot in the sock.

2. Place the scale on the floor.

3. Hold the sock just above the scale.

4. Drop the sock on the scale and note how far the scale needle moves.

5. Repeat step 4, holding the sock about waist high above the scale.

Results The scale needle moves farther when the sock is dropped from a higher position.

Why? The gravitational potential energy of an object is equal to the work done to raise the object, and assuming no friction with air as it falls, the gravitational potential energy is equal to the work the object can do when it drops from its raised position. The work done to raise the sock is equal to the force weight of the sock times its height above the scale.

As the height increases, more work is done to raise the sock, so the gravitational potential energy of the sock increases. This is demonstrated by the movement of the scale needle. The needle moved more when the scale was struck by the sock dropped from a higher position because more work was done on the scale by this sock than by the sock dropped from a lower height.

Solutions to Exercises

1a. *Think!*

- The weight of the object is 40 pounds.

- The height the object was raised is 6 feet.

- The equation to determine gravitational potential energy is:

$$GPE = f_{wt} \times h$$
$$= 40 \text{ lb} \times 6 \text{ ft} \quad (180 \text{ N} \times 1.8 \text{ m})$$
$$= 240 \text{ ft-lb} \quad (324 \text{ joules})$$

The gravitational potential energy of the object is 240 ft-lb (324 joules).

b. *Think!*

- If friction is not considered, the gravitational potential energy of an object equals the work it can do.

- The gravitational potential energy of the object is 240 ft-lb (324 joules).

The work the object can do when it falls is 240 ft-lb (324 joules).

2a. *Think!*

- Chemical potential energy is energy stored in the bonds that hold atoms together.

- Food contains chemical energy that is released when you eat it.

- Fuel contains chemical energy that is released when it is burned.

Figures A and C represent chemical potential energy.

b. Think!

- Gravitational potential energy is the energy of an object raised above a surface.

- Which figure has an object raised above a surface? The bag is raised above the floor in figure B.

Figure B represents gravitational potential energy.

3. Think!

- Elastic potential energy is energy stored by an object that is in a state of being stretched or twisted.

A stretched rubber band represents elastic potential energy.

5

On the Move

Kinetic Energy

What You Need to Know

The energy that a moving object has because of its motion is called kinetic energy. A moving object can do work on another object by colliding with that object and moving it. For example, a falling rock does work when it hits the ground and mashes the ground down. So objects have kinetic energy because they are moving.

If a ball that is moving very slowly hits a glass window, the work done by the ball on the glass may not be enough to break the glass. But if the same ball moving at a high speed hits the window, the work done by the ball on the glass most likely will be enough to cause the glass to break. The faster an object moves, the greater its kinetic energy and the more work it does on any object it hits.

The amount of kinetic energy of an object depends on its **velocity** (speed in a particular direction). But, all objects moving at the same velocity do not have the same kinetic energy. For example, think of the effect that a rolling marble would have on bowling pins. Compare this with the pins being hit by a bowling ball rolling at the same speed as the marble. The effect of the bowling ball is more noticeable than the marble. So the ball has more kinetic energy. This is because the ball has more mass (amount of material in a substance). So the amount of kinetic energy depends on the mass of an object as well as its velocity.

The relationship between kinetic energy (KE), mass (m), and velocity (v) can be expressed by the equation:

$$KE = \tfrac{1}{2}\,mv^2$$

According to the equation, an increase in either the mass or velocity of an object increases the object's kinetic energy. But since the velocity in the equation is **squared** (multiplied by itself), it has the greater effect on kinetic energy. The common metric unit for energy is joule (J) if the mass is measured in kilograms (kg) and the velocity in meters per second (m/s). For example, an object with a mass of 1 kg and a speed of 2 m/s has a kinetic energy of 2 J.

$$
\begin{aligned}
KE &= \tfrac{1}{2}\,mv^2 \\
&= \tfrac{1}{2}\,(1\ \text{kg})\,(2\ \text{m/s})^2 \\
&= \tfrac{1}{2}\,(1\ \text{kg})\,(2\ \text{m/s})\,(2\ \text{m/s}) \\
&= 2\ \text{kg m}^2/\text{s}^2 \\
&= 2\ \text{J}
\end{aligned}
$$

Note that when a number is squared, such as $(2 \text{ m/s})^2$, the number as well as its units are multiplied by themselves: $(2 \text{ m/s})^2 = (2 \text{ m/s})(2 \text{ m/s}) = 4 \text{ m}^2/\text{s}^2$. Also note that the units can be grouped, forming $\text{kg m}^2/\text{s}^2$. Since $1 \text{ kg m}^2/\text{s}^2 = 1 \text{ J}$, $2 \text{ kg m}^2/\text{s}^2 = 2 \text{ J}$.

Exercises

1. In the figure, which has more kinetic energy, the boy or the dog?

2. How many joules of energy are needed to move a 3-kg object at a velocity of 4 m/s?

Activity: SWINGER

Purpose   To demonstrate the effect of velocity on kinetic energy.

Materials   1 cup dry rice
sock
3-foot (0.9-m) piece of string
sheet of copy paper

transparent tape
unopened can of food
pencil

Procedure

1. Pour the rice in the sock and tie a knot in the sock.

2. Tie one end of the string around the knot in the sock.

3. Tape the free end of the string to the top edge of a table. Adjust the length of the string by pulling on it so that the sock hangs about 1 inch (2.5 cm) above the floor. Then place one or more pieces of tape over the string to hold it in place.

4. Tape the paper to the floor underneath the sock so that the sock hangs above the edge of the paper.

5. Set the can of food on the edge of the paper so that its side touches the sock.

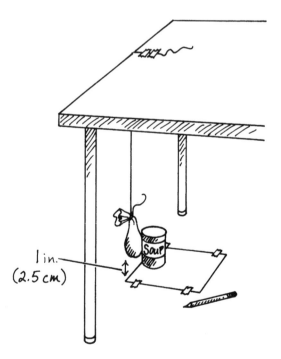

6. Pull the sock about 2 inches (5 cm) away from the can.

7. Release the sock and allow it to hit the can.

8. With the pencil, mark on the paper the edge of the can closest to the sock.

9. Repeat steps 6 through 8 two or more times, but pull the sock farther away from the can each time.

Results The farther the sock is pulled away from the can of food, the farther the can is moved.

Why? The hanging sock is an example of a **pendulum**, which is a suspended weight that is free to swing back and forth. The weight and therefore the mass of the sock remained the same. The change was in the height of the sock. As the height of the sock increased, the velocity of the sock increased. Since the kinetic energy of the swinging sock depends on the sock's mass and its velocity, the kinetic energy increases as the height of the sock increases. This was shown by an increase in the distance the can moved when hit by the swinging sock. With more kinetic energy, the sock does more work on the can, thus moving it a farther distance.

Solutions to Exercises

1. *Think!*

- The kinetic energy of an object depends on the mass of the object and its velocity. As the mass and/or velocity increases, the kinetic energy increases.

- The boy and the dog are moving at the same velocity.

- The boy has more mass than the dog.

The boy has more mass than the dog; therefore, the boy has more kinetic energy.

2. *Think!*

- The equation for calculating kinetic energy is:

  KE = ½ *mv*²

- When a value is squared, the number is multiplied by itself.

So the kinetic energy of the object is:
  KE = ½ (3 kg) (4 m/s) (4 m/s)

- If the mass is measured in kilograms and the velocity in meters per second, the energy is measured in joules.

The kinetic energy of the object is 24 joules.

6

Sum It Up

The Law of Conservation of Mechanical Energy

What You Need to Know

Mechanical energy (ME) is energy of motion regardless of whether that energy is in action or stored. Mechanical energy is the sum of the kinetic and potential energy of an object. In other words, it is the sum of **mechanical kinetic energy** (a form of mechanical energy in which the energy of an object is due to the motion of the object) and mechanical potential energy (a form of mechanical energy in which the energy of an object is due to its position or condition).

All kinetic energy is mechanical energy, but all mechanical energy is not kinetic energy. Some mechanical energy is potential energy. There are different forms of potential energy, including chemical and mechanical. Chemical potential energy describes the potential energy stored in the bonds holding atoms together. Mechanical potential energy describes the potential energy of an object that is capable of motion because of its position or condition. A compressed spring is an example of mechanical potential energy.

An object can have both mechanical potential energy and mechanical kinetic energy at the same time. For example, when a ball is dropped, it starts to fall. As the ball falls, more and more of its potential energy is transferred to kinetic energy. The **law of conservation of mechanical energy** states that the sum of the mechanical potential energy and

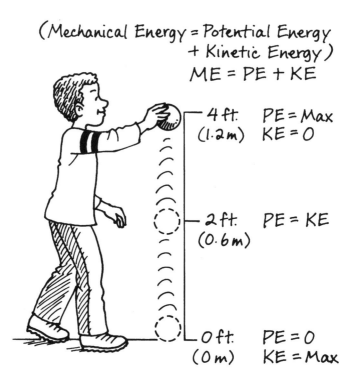

(*Mechanical Energy = Potential Energy + Kinetic Energy*)

ME = PE + KE

4 ft. (1.2 m)   PE = Max   KE = 0

2 ft. (0.6 m)   PE = KE

0 ft. (0 m)   PE = 0   KE = Max

the mechanical kinetic energy of an object remains the same as long as no outside force, such as friction, acts on it. So before the ball is dropped, it has maximum potential energy and zero kinetic energy. Halfway through the fall, the potential and kinetic energy are equal. When the ball strikes the ground, it has maximum kinetic energy and zero potential energy.

Exercises

1. Study the figures and determine which figure, A or B, represents:

a. mechanical potential energy

b. mechanical kinetic energy

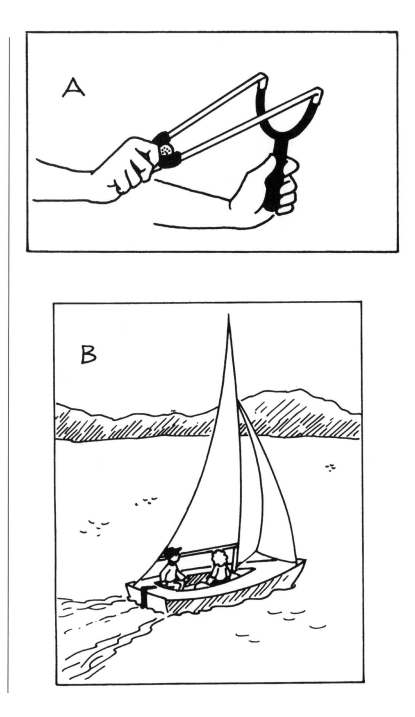

2. Which position in the figure, A, B, or C, shows the child with both mechanical potential and mechanical kinetic energy?

Activity: MAGIC CAN

Purpose To demonstrate how friction affects the change between mechanical potential and mechanical kinetic energy.

Materials 2 plastic coffee can lids
13-ounce (368-g) coffee can, empty, with top and
   bottom removed
pencil
3- to 4-inch (7.5- to 10-cm)–long rubber band
2 paper clips
10 pennies
masking tape

Procedure

1. Place the lids on the ends of the can.

2. Use the pencil to make a hole in the center of each lid. The holes should be large enough for the rubber band to go through.

3. Remove the lids from the can.

4. Thread one end of the rubber band through each hole from the inside of the lids. Clip one of the paper clips to each end of the rubber band to keep it from pulling back through the lid. Pull on the rubber band to pull the paper clips snugly against the lids. The insides of the lids should be facing each other.

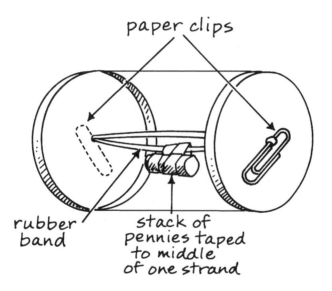

paper clips

rubber band

stack of pennies taped to middle of one strand

5. Stack the coins and wrap tape around them. Use tape to secure the stack of coins to the middle of one strand of the rubber band.

6. Slightly fold one of the lids and push it inside the can.

7. Snap the other lid over one end of the can, then pull the lid inside the can out and snap it in place at the other end.

Note: If the coins touch the side of the can, tighten the rubber band by pulling its ends through one lid and tying a knot in them. Adjust the coins so that they stay in the center.

8. Place the can on its side on the floor and push the can so that its rolls forward. Observe the motion of the can until it stops moving. Note: The can needs about 10 feet (3 m) or more for rolling.

Results The can rolls forward and stops, then rolls backward and stops again. Some cans roll back and forth several times.

Why? You do work on the can by pushing it. This work gives the can mechanical kinetic energy, so it rolls across the floor. As the can rolls, the rubber band winds up, storing more and more potential energy. This energy is called elastic potential energy, which is a form of mechanical potential energy. When the can stops, the rubber band starts to unwind, and the elastic potential energy stored in it is changed to mechanical kinetic energy, causing the can to roll backward. The can continues to roll after the rubber band is unwound due to **inertia** (the tendency of an object in motion to continue to move forward), causing the rubber band to wind up again. This winding and unwinding of the rubber band can continue several times until all the mechanical kinetic energy is transferred into other types of energy, mostly heat from friction. Then the can stops.

Solutions to Exercises

1a. *Think!*

- Mechanical potential energy is stored energy that can cause an object as a whole to move.

- The rubber band on the slingshot is stretched. If

released, the energy in the stretched rubber band will do work on the rock, causing it to move forward.

Figure A represents an object with mechanical potential energy.

b. **Think!**

- Mechanical kinetic energy is the energy in a moving object.

- The boat is moving across the water.

Figure B represents an object with mechanical kinetic energy.

2. **Think!**

- In position A, the child is not moving, but he will move when he stops holding on. So he has mechanical potential energy.

- In position B, part of the potential energy has been changed to kinetic energy.

- In position C, there is zero potential energy and maximum kinetic energy.

The child has both mechanical potential and mechanical kinetic energy in position B.

7

Disturbances

Mechanical Waves

What You Need to Know

A **wave** is a traveling disturbance that transfers energy, but not matter, from one place to another. Waves that require a medium are called **mechanical waves**. Water is a medium for water waves and air is the common medium for sound waves. Waves that do not require a medium and can travel through **space** (region beyond Earth's atmosphere) are called **electromagnetic waves**. Energy, such as light and heat, traveling in the form of electromagnetic waves is called **radiation** or **radiant energy**. All the different types of radiation arranged in order from low-energy radio waves to high-energy X-rays are known as the **electromagnetic spectrum**. For more information about radiant energy, see chapter 11. Tapping the surface of water at regular intervals with your finger several times produces evenly spaced ripples that spread out in circles from the place where your finger disturbed the water. **Ripples** are disturbances in a substance called a **medium** through which waves travel. Ripples following each other at regular intervals are called **periodic waves** or simply **waves**. You made the waves by moving your finger up and down several times. Any motion that repeatedly follows the same path, such as a side-to-side or up-and-down motion, is called a **vibration**. All waves are produced by some vibrating source, such as the tapping of your finger on the water. A stone dropped in the water causes the water to repeatedly move down and up in one spot, thus sending out waves from the vibrating spot.

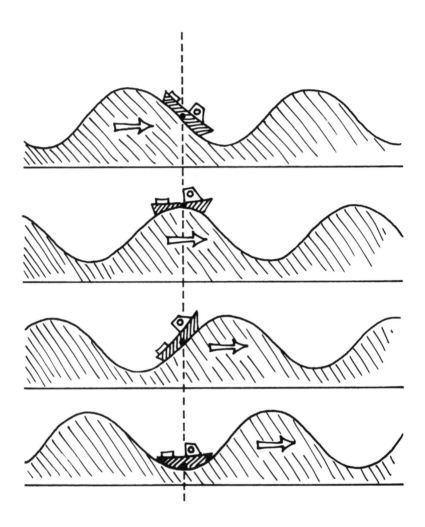

As waves move across the surface of water, it looks like the water is moving outward, but it isn't. Instead, only the wave is moving forward. This can be proved by floating an object, such as a toy boat, on the water. Waves will cause the boat to bob up and down but not move toward shore. The waves pass the boat and move forward, but the boat remains in approximately the same place.

There are two types of mechanical waves based on the direction of the **displacement** (to take out of normal position) of the medium compared to the direction of the wave motion: transverse waves and longitudinal waves. In a **transverse wave**, the medium displacement is perpendicular to the motion of the wave. So if the disturbance is vertical, such as a water wave, the wave motion is horizontal. Water waves as well as all electromagnetic waves are transverse waves. In a **longitudinal wave**, the medium displacement is parallel to the wave motion. So if the disturbance is horizontal, the wave motion is also horizontal. These waves, such as sound waves, cause **compression** (squeezing together) and **rarefaction** (spreading out) of the medium.

Transverse and longitudinal waves have the same basic characteristics: amplitude, wavelength, and frequency. The maximum movement of the particles of a medium from their resting position is called the **amplitude**. As the energy of a wave increases, so does its amplitude. The **wavelength** of one wave is the distance that can be measured from any point

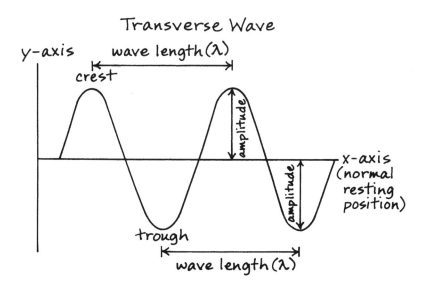

on one wave to the same point on the consecutive wave. **Frequency** is the number of waves per unit of time. The metric unit of **hertz (Hz)** is commonly used to measure frequency. A frequency of one hertz equals one wave per second.

A line graph can be used to represent transverse wave characteristics. The up-and-down pattern of the graph represents amplitude.

The x-axis of the graph represents the resting or normal position of the medium before the disturbance. The y-axis represents the disturbance. In a transverse wave, the amount of movement from rest is shown by the distance above and below the resting position—the x-axis. The high points of the graph above the x-axis represent the **crests** (the high part of transverse waves). The low parts of the graph represent the **troughs**. Basically, one crest and one trough make up one transverse wave. The symbol for wavelength is the Greek letter lambda (λ).

In a longitudinal wave, the particles of the material vibrate back and forth in a direction parallel to the motion of the

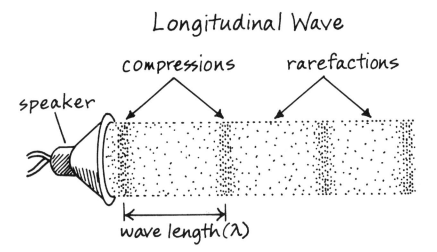

wave. This causes the particles of the medium to be squeezed together, then pulled apart, forming compressions and rarefactions respectively. The amplitude of a longitudinal wave is determined by **density** (the number of particles in an area). The greater the amplitude, the more **dense** (parts are close together) are the compression regions and the less dense are the rarefaction regions. One compression and one rarefaction make up one wave.

Exercises

1. Which figure A, or B, represents a mechanical wave?

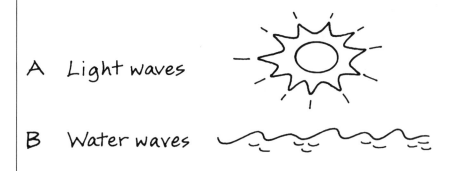

A Light waves

B Water waves

2. The following questions refer to wave figures A, B, and C on page 54:

   a. Which figure, A, B, or C, has waves with the longest wavelength?

   b. If each figure represents a period of time of 1 second, which figure, A, B, or C, represents a wave with the greatest frequency?

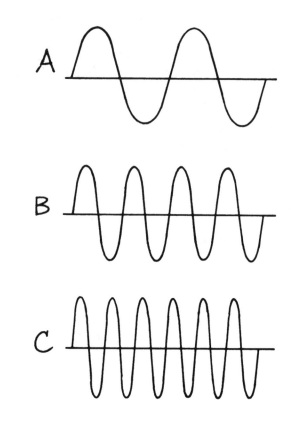

Activity: **BOUNCING**

Purpose   To demonstrate how mechanical wave energy is transferred.

Materials   box with one side at least 10 inches (25 cm) long
20 to 30 grains of rice
pencil

Procedure

1. Set the box on a table.

2. Spread the grains of rice in a row across the top of the box.

3. With the eraser end of the pencil, gently tap on the top of the box near one end of the row of rice grains. Observe the movement of the rice grains.

4. Repeat step 3, but tap harder.

Results When the box is tapped gently, all or most of the rice grains slowly bounce around, staying in about the same position on the box. Harder tapping causes the rice grains to quickly bounce around. Some lift off the box, moving to different places. The grains all appear to move at the same time, and the ones near the pencil move more.

Why? Each tap pushes the box down when the pencil hits. Thus, work is done on the box and energy is transferred to it. The repeated tapping disturbs the surface of the box, sending a mechanical wave across the surfaces of the box. The direction of the medium (box) disturbance is vertical (up and down) and the motion of the wave is horizontal (across the box). The wave moves so quickly that the rice grains appear to move at the same time. The grains near where the pencil taps move more, because as a wave moves away from the source producing it, energy of the wave is lost. Some of the energy is transferred to the grains of rice, some to air above the box, and some to the box itself. The grains bounce up and down but generally stay in the same position, because the wave moving across the box carries energy, not material. So the grains are just temporarily disturbed from their original resting position but return to the approximate resting position when the wave passes. If the grains receive enough energy to be lifted above the box's surface, they may fall in a new location. This is because when the pencil is tapped hard against the box, it gives the wave more energy to transfer to the rice. Unlike water molecules, the rice grains are not connected and can move independently of one another, so they can fly off the box.

Solutions to Exercises

1. *Think!*

- Mechanical waves move through a medium, which is any kind of matter, such as water.

- Light waves are a form of electromagnetic waves, which do not require a medium.

Figure B, water waves, represents mechanical waves.

2a. *Think!*

- Wavelength is from the point of one wave to the same point on a consecutive wave.

- Which wave has a greater distance between two points on consecutive waves?

Figure A has waves with the longest wavelength.

b. *Think!*

- The frequency of a wave is the number of waves in a given amount of time.

- Figure A has two waves, figure B has four waves, and figure C has six waves.

- What figure has the most waves per second?

Figure C, with six waves per second, has the greatest frequency.

8

Up and Down

Energy Movement in Transverse Waves

What You Need to Know

In a transverse wave, the displacement medium moves perpendicular to the motion of the wave (see chapter 7). Waves can change direction if they hit a barrier in their path. The barrier can **absorb** (take in) and **reflect** (bounce back from a surface) the energy of the wave. For example, if one end of a rope is secured to a tree, a wave moving along the rope will be reflected by the tree. A small amount of the wave energy will be absorbed by the tree, but most will travel back along the rope as a reflected wave.

When two sets of waves with the same frequency and wavelength moving in opposite directions meet, they form **standing waves** (waves that appear to remain still). Standing waves do not appear to move through the medium. Instead, the waves cause the medium to vibrate in a series of loops. Note in the figure that each half of a wave moves up and down, and points called **nodes** along the wave are not displaced from the resting position. The crests and troughs of a standing wave are called **antinodes**.

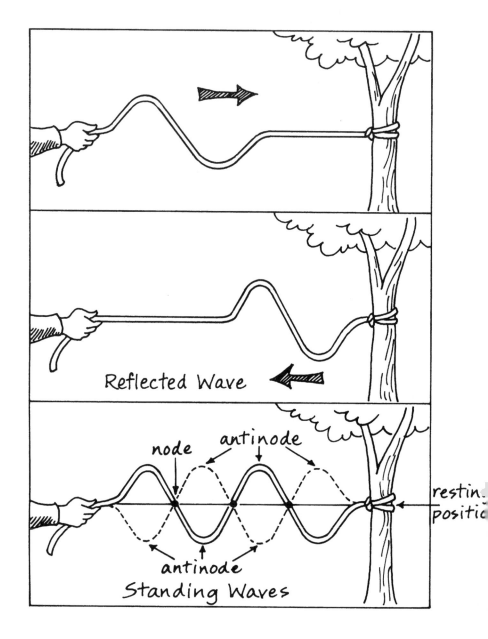

Exercises

1. Each set in the Wave Data table contains the medium disturbance direction and the direction of the wave. Which set, A, B, or C, describes a transverse wave?

Wave Data

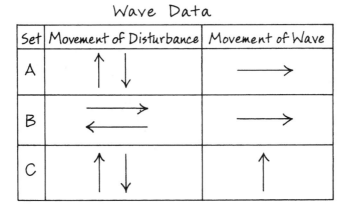

Set	Movement of Disturbance	Movement of Wave
A	↑ ↓	⟶
B	⟶ ⟵	⟶
C	↑ ↓	↑

2. In the figure, which part of the standing wave, A or B, is a node?

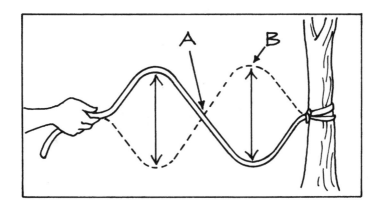

Activity: STANDING

Purpose To determine how the frequency of a vibrating source affects the standing waves produced.

Materials   paper towel
transparent tape
12-inch (30-cm) piece of string
Slinky

Procedure

1. Fold the paper towel in half three times and wrap it around the bottom of a chair leg. Secure the paper towel by wrapping a piece of tape around it. The paper towel is used to protect the surface of the chair leg.

2. Stretch the Slinky out on the floor to a length of about 6 to 8 feet (1.8 to 2.4 m). Use the string to tie one end of the slinky to the chair leg over the paper towel.

3. Holding the free end of the Slinky, quickly move the end from side to side one time to send a wave down the spring. Observe the motion of the wave.

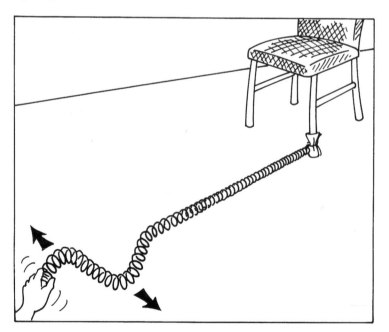

4. Slowly move the end of the Slinky from side to side, changing the number of side-to-side motions until

standing waves are formed. Try to move the end the same distance each time.

5. Repeat step 4, but quickly move the end of the Slinky from side to side.

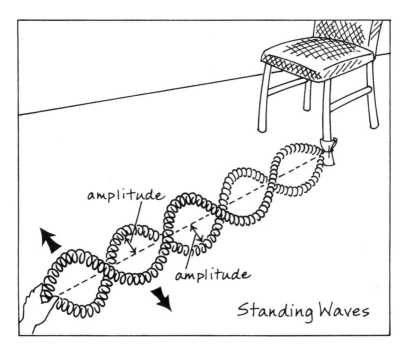

Results As the speed of the side-to-side motion of the end of the Slinky increases, the number of standing waves increases.

Why? A wave that does not appear to be moving, is a standing wave. Points on the wave called nodes stay in place while areas between the nodes move back and forth, alternately forming crests and troughs called antinodes with each motion. In this experiment, standing waves were formed by vibrating the end of a Slinky. The frequency of vibration increased as the speed of the side-to-side motion increased. As the frequency of the vibrating source (the end of the Slinky) increased, the number of standing waves increased.

Solutions to Exercises

1. *Think!*

- The direction of the displacement of a transverse wave is perpendicular to the direction of the wave.

- Which set, A, B, or C, shows movement of displacement perpendicular to wave motion?

Set A represents the displacement and wave motion in a transverse wave.

2. *Think!*

- A node is the part of a standing wave that does not move away from the resting position (the horizontal line).

- Which part of the figure, A or B, does not indicate motion above or below the resting position?

In the figure, part A is a node.

9

Back and Forth

Sound Energy

What You Need to Know

Sound energy is mechanical energy (energy of motion) transferred as a wave by vibrating particles. **Sound waves** are longitudinal waves produced by sound energy in which there are compressions (crowded parts) and rarefactions (uncrowded parts) of the particles of the medium through which the waves move. A stretched Slinky can be used to model sound waves moving through a material. If some of the Slinky's coils at one end are squeezed together, an area of compression is produced that causes the coils in front of them to spread out. The compression of the coils creates a region of rarefaction. When the squeezed coils are released, they move apart, pushing the coils in front of them together. In turn, these compressed coils move forward, pushing on the coils in front of them, and so on. Compressing the end coils gives them energy that is transferred from one end of the Slinky to the other. As the wave of energy goes through the Slinky, all the coils do not move at once, so some of them are crowded together and some are spread apart.

A sound wave originates when an object vibrates (moves back and forth or to and fro). In turn, this vibration causes compression and rarefaction of air particles similar to that in the Slinky. The individual air particles that carry the sound energy move back and forth parallel to the direction of

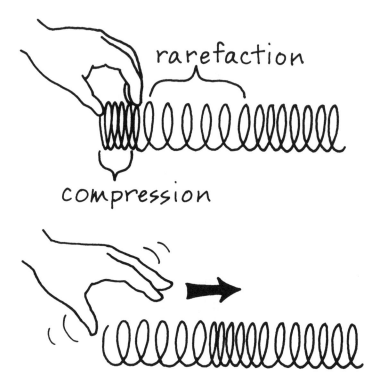

wave motion. Thus, a sound wave is a series of alternate compressions and rarefactions of air particles. Each individual particle passes the energy on to neighboring particles, but after the sound wave has passed, like the Slinky coils, each air particle remains in about the same location.

Each time any part of an object vibrates, sound waves are sent out in all directions. As the object continues to vibrate, a train of sound waves moves away from the object. The faster the object vibrates, the faster the sound waves are produced and thus the greater is the wave's frequency. **Pitch** is the measure of how high or low a sound is to an observer, and it is determined by the sound's frequency. The greater the frequency, the higher the pitch. The loudness of a sound depends on the energy of the sound wave. As the energy increases, the amplitude (amount of distance the particles are moved from their resting position) of the sound wave increases. The energy of sound waves depends on several things, including the distance from the vibrating source as well as how spread out the waves are. As the distance and spreading out of the waves increase, the energy and loudness decrease.

When sound waves in air enter your ears, special cells are moved that send messages to your brain. Your brain interprets the messages as **sound**. The more energy a sound wave has, the louder the sound is heard. Sound waves are mechanical waves, meaning a medium is necessary. If there is no medium, there is no sound. For example, there is no sound in space (region beyond Earth's atmosphere) because there is relatively no medium in space. Most of the sounds that we hear travel in air. But sound can also travel in liquids and solids. Sound travels most rapidly in solids, and more rapidly in liquids than in gases. For example, Native Americans used to put their ears to the ground to listen for sounds of bison herds (or buffalo). They could hear the sound sooner through the ground than through the air because the speed of sound in the solid ground is about four times as fast as in the air.

Exercises

1. In the sound wave moving away from the ringing bell, which part, A or B, represents the following parts of a longitudinal wave:

   a. compression

   b. rarefaction

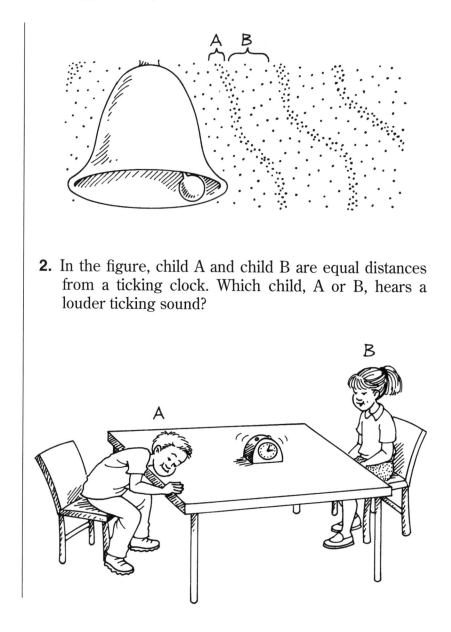

2. In the figure, child A and child B are equal distances from a ticking clock. Which child, A or B, hears a louder ticking sound?

Activity: ASTRO SOUNDS

Purpose To determine how amplitudes affect the loudness of sound.

Materials   metal Slinky
16-ounce (480-ml) plastic cup

Procedure

1. Stick one end of the Slinky into the bottom of the cup.

2. Stand with the open end of the cup over one ear and the Slinky stretched so that its free end rests on the floor. Lean slightly so that the Slinky is as straight as possible and not touching your body.

3. With your hand, squeeze three or four coils of the Slinky together near the bottom of the cup, then release the coils. Note the loudness of the sound produced.

4. Repeat step 3, but compress eight or more coils together.

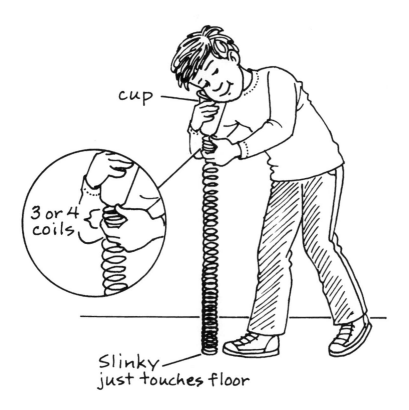

Results A louder sound is heard when more coils are compressed together.

Why? The sound bounces back and forth as the waves move through the springs of the Slinky and reflect off the bottom of the cup and the floor. When you compress more coils together, you hear a louder sound because you have put more energy into the sound. Loudness is related to the amount of energy carried by a wave. The amplitude of a wave is an indication of its energy; the greater the energy, the greater the amplitude. For sound waves, this means the compressions are more crowded and the rarefactions are more spread out. The greater the amplitude of a sound, the louder the sound.

A scale of sound **intensities** (sound wave energy per second) has been developed with an intensity unit of **decibels (dB)**. A decibel of 0 is a sound so soft it can barely be heard. Whispering is about 10 dB, normal conversation is 60 to 70 dB, loud music is about 90 to 100 dB, a jet engine is about 100 dB, and pain is caused by a sound intensity greater than about 120 dB.

Solutions to Exercises

1a. *Think!*

- The vibrating bell produces sound waves, which are longitudinal waves.

- Compression is the part of a longitudinal wave where particles of the matter through which the wave moves are crowded together.

- Which area, A or B, shows air particles crowded together?

Area A represents compression in a sound wave.

b. *Think!*

- Rarefaction is the part of a longitudinal wave where particles of the matter through which the wave moves are spread apart or are less crowded together.

- Which area, A or B, shows air particles spread apart?

Area B represents rarefaction in a sound wave.

2. *Think!*

- Because of the table's size, sound traveling through it does not spread out as much as it does when traveling through air.

- Sound waves lose more energy when they spread out. The sound waves can spread out more in the air than in the table.

- Sound is louder when it has more energy, so sound traveling through the table is louder.

- Which child is listening to the ticking sound traveling through the table?

Child A hears a louder ticking sound.

10
Energy Bundles
Photons

What You Need to Know

The energy of the electrons of an atom is compared by a model called energy levels. **Energy levels** are regions around and at different distances from the atom's nucleus. The energy of electrons is different in each energy level, with those farthest from the nucleus having the most energy. Energy levels can be compared to a ladder. A person can climb from one rung to another but cannot stand between the rungs. In a similar manner, electrons move from one energy level to another but do not stop in between.

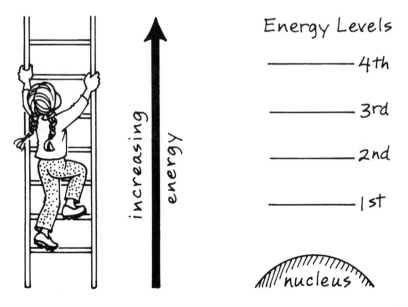

Ground state is the normal (lowest) energy level of a specific electron in an atom. When an electron absorbs a specific amount of energy, it "jumps" to a higher energy level farther from the nucleus. With this extra energy, the electron is **unstable** (likely to change) and said to be in an **excited state** (the energy level of an electron in an atom that is greater than its ground state). Electrons remain in an excited state for only a few billionths of a second before emitting the extra energy and returning to its ground state.

The energy gained by an electron can come from different sources, including electricity, heat, light, and high-energy ultraviolet radiation (UV). But the extra energy of an electron in an excited state is generally released as light. Light exists as packets of energy called **photons**, which are a quantity of electromagnetic energy. The wavelength of a particular color of light is an indication of its photons. **Visible light** is radiation that the human eye can see. The **visible spectrum** is visible light arranged in order from highest to lowest wavelength includes red, orange, yellow, green, blue, indigo, and violet. As the wavelength of any radiation decreases, the energy of the radiation increases. Thus, red light with a larger wavelength has less energy than violet light. Each color of light has photons with the same amount of energy. When an electron releases photons, the color of the visible light depends on the amount of energy of the released photon.

The hotter a material is heated, the higher the energy level of the excited state of the electrons and the greater the energy of the released photons. So the color of a heated material can be used to indicate temperature. A blue flame caused by the release of "blue" photons is much hotter than a yellow flame resulting from the release of lesser-energy "yellow" photons.

The color of stars gives an indication of how hot the stars are. Stars are grouped into **spectral types** indicating their color and temperature. A letter is assigned to each type. In order of decreasing surface temperature, the letters are OBAFGKM. The famous **mnemonic** (memory device) used to remember these letters in order is "Oh Be A Fine Girl (Guy), Kiss Me." The chart lists the basic color of stars for each type. Note that types O and B are both blue, but they are not the same shade of blue. O is hotter and therefore is more of a blue-violet. It takes a special instrument called a **spectroscope** (instrument used to separate light into separate colors) to distinguish between the colors of some stars.

Spectral Types

Type	Color
O	blue
B	blue
A	blue-white
F	white
G	yellow
K	orange
M	orange-red

The color of a heated material is also affected by the elements in it. While yellow stars have a temperature of 10,000°F (5,538°C), a fire log can burn at a much lower temperature and produce a yellow flame because there is an abundance of the element carbon in the log. Carbon produces a yellow flame when heated. Other elements can be identified by the color of light they give off when heated, such as pale green for barium and red for lithium. These and other chemicals are used to coat fire logs to produce a multicolored flame.

Exercises

1. Use the Spectral Types chart on page 75 and the diagram below of the Gemini **constellation** (a group of stars that appear to form a pattern) to answer the following:

   a. How many of the labeled stars are yellow?

   b. Which are the coolest stars?

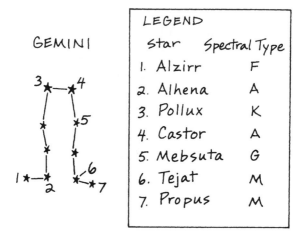

GEMINI

LEGEND

Star	Spectral Type
1. Alzirr	F
2. Alhena	A
3. Pollux	K
4. Castor	A
5. Mebsuta	G
6. Tejat	M
7. Propus	M

2. Level 1 is the ground state of the electron in figures A and B. Use the figures to answer the following:

   a. Which figure, A or B, shows the electron of the atom in an excited state?

   b. Which figure, A or B, shows the electron in a position in which it can emit light?

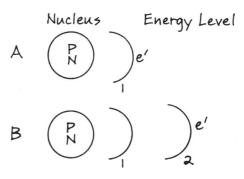

Activity: BRIGHTER

Purpose   To show that excited electrons give off light when they lose energy.

Materials   scissors
newsprint
white index card
transparent tape
fluorescent yellow highlighter pen
incandescent lamp

Procedure

1. Cut a piece of newsprint slightly smaller than the index card.

2. Secure the newsprint to the card with tape.

3. Use the pen to highlight part of the print on the card.

4. Hold the card so that the light from the incandescent lamp shines on it. Make note of the brightness of the highlighted areas on the card.

5. Repeat step 4 using sunlight.

Results The highlighted area is brighter when viewed in sunlight.

Why? Fluorescent ink has a special chemical that absorbs invisible ultraviolet radiation and changes it to visible light that is the same color as the ink. This happens because electrons in the chemical absorb ultraviolet radiation, causing some of the electrons in the chemical to be excited. The excited electrons lose their excess energy in the form of photons of visible light. Thus, the ink is absorbing invisible radiation and emitting visible light of the same color as the ink. For yellow fluorescent ink, yellow photons are emitted. Yellow fluorescent ink has yellow pigment that reflects yellow photons from visible light striking it, plus the special chemical that absorbs UV radiation and emits yellow light. With this combined yellow light, the ink is extra bright in color. If the ink is viewed in visible light only, such as light produced by an incandescent lamp, the ink looks yellow because of the reflected yellow light, but it is not an extra bright yellow. Also, some incandescent light gives off a slighly yellow color, making the card appear yellowish. Thus, the area highlighted with the yellow ink may blend in with the yellowed paper, making it difficult to see.

Solutions to Exercises

1a. *Think!*

- What spectral type is yellow? G

- Which stars in the diagram are type G? One star is type G, Mebsuta.

There is one yellow star in the diagram of Gemini, Mebsuta.

b. *Think!*

- Which spectral type is the coolest? M

- What are the names of the type M stars?

Propus and Tejat are the coolest stars in the diagram of Gemini.

2a. *Think!*

- Electrons at ground state are at their lowest energy level. Those in an excited state are at a higher energy level.

- The ground state of the electrons in figures A and B is level 1.

- Which diagram shows the electron at an energy level greater than level 1?

Figure B shows the electron of the atom in an excited state.

b. *Think!*

- Excited electrons can give off photons when they return to the ground state.

- Photons are bundles of light energy.

- Which figure shows an excited electron? B

Figure B shows an electron that can give off light.

11
Through Space
Radiant Energy

What You Need to Know

Radiant energy travels in the form of electromagnetic waves. The source of any wave is a vibration. For example, a vibrating drum causes air particles around it to vibrate, producing sound waves. These waves are mechanical waves that require a medium, which is generally air. But electromagnetic waves do not need a medium, which means they can travel through space, the region outside Earth's atmosphere that is relatively without a medium.

The sources of mechanical waves are vibrating particles of a medium, and the sources of electromagnetic waves are vibrating electrons that create an **electric field** (region where there is a push or pull on an electric charge) and a **magnetic field** (region where there is a push or pull on magnetic material). These fields vibrate at right angles to each other and to the direction of motion. Thus, electromagnetic waves are transverse waves.

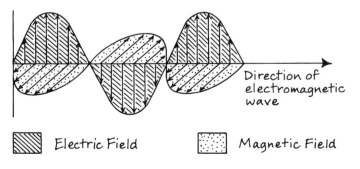

Direction of electromagnetic wave

Electric Field   Magnetic Field

Since a medium is not required for radiant energy to move from one place to another, **solar energy** (radiant energy from the Sun) can travel from the Sun through space to reach Earth. All forms of radiant energy travel at a speed of 186,000 miles (300 million meters) per second in a vacuum. This speed is called the **speed of light**. So solar energy traveling at the speed of light can reach Earth, which is about 93 million miles (149 million km) away, in about 8 minutes.

The different types of radiant energy are arranged in order of their wavelengths in the electromagnetic spectrum. The electromagnetic spectrum, from the shortest wavelength and most energetic type of radiation to the longest wavelength and least energetic type of radiation, includes gamma rays, X-rays, ultraviolet radiation, visible light, infrared radiation, microwaves, and radio waves.

Gamma rays and **X-rays** are invisible radiation produced in nuclear reactions and can pass through most substances. Gamma rays are used by doctors to kill cancer cells. X-rays can pass through human tissue but not bones, so doctors use them to take special pictures of the bones in your body.

Ultraviolet radiation (UV) is an invisible radiation given off by very hot objects, such as the Sun. UV is produced by special lightbulbs, including black lights and sun lamps, and small amounts of UV radiation are produced by fluorescent lightbulbs. Ultraviolet radiation is used for the **sterilization** (a process that kills bacteria)of objects. UV also causes **tanning** (the process of turning the skin darker), but excess UV causes sunburn and can cause skin cancer. You should limit the time you spend in the sunshine, cover your body, wear sunglasses to protect your eyes, and use sunblock lotions on your skin that help block UV rays.

Following ultraviolet radiation is violet light, the most energetic part of the visible spectrum. All radiant energy is invisible except for visible light. Solar energy contains all forms of radiant energy, but the radiation reaching Earth's surface is mainly visible light. A combination of all the colored light in the visible spectrum produces **white light**. Chemicals in objects that give them color are called **pigments**. The color of an object depends on what part of the visible spectrum the pigments in the object absorb and what part is reflected (bounced back from a surface) to your eye. For example, when white light hits an apple, the apple looks red because all of the light making up the visible spectrum is absorbed except red light, which is reflected to your eye.

Infrared radiation (IR) follows visible red light, the least energetic light in the visible spectrum. When infrared radiation hits an object, it is transformed into kinetic energy, causing the particles in the object to vibrate more rapidly, thus increasing its temperature. Infrared radiation is so effective at heating an object that it is often called **radiant heat**. For more information about infrared radiation, see chapter 14.

Next in line on the electromagnetic spectrum are two of the largest, but least energetic waves, **microwaves** followed by **radio waves**. Microwaves are absorbed by some materials, such as water and fat in foods, but pass through other materials, such as paper plates. For more information about materials that absorb or allow radiation to pass through, see chapter 14. In a microwave oven, the microwaves cause water and fat molecules in food to rapidly flip back and forth. The moving molecules bounce into one another. Much like quickly rubbing your hands together causes them to feel hot, the friction of the molecules bouncing into one another causes food in microwave ovens to get hot. Microwaves and radio waves are both used in communication, carrying signals that you hear as sound and see as pictures on radios and televisions.

Exercises

1. Study the figure to answer the following questions:

  a. What is the common name for the energy the girl is receiving from the Sun?

  b. What part of the Sun's energy causes tanning and in excess could cause harm to the girl's body?

  c. The girl is wearing shades to protect her eyes from excessive UV rays. What else can she do to protect her body from the Sun's energy?

2. Study the figure on page 85 to answer the following questions:

  a. What is the name of the radiant energy source for the white light?

  b. What color would the flower in the figure appear to be?

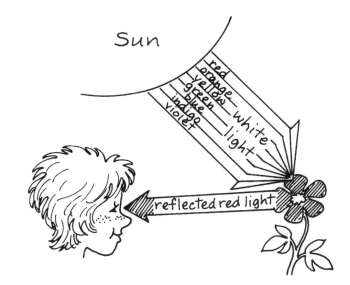

Activity: LIGHT PAINTING

Purpose   To demonstrate reflection of light.

Materials   sheet of white copy paper
flashlight
2 pieces of construction paper—1 yellow, 1 red

Procedure

1. Fold the white paper in half from top to bottom.

2. Stand the paper on a table. This will be your screen.

3. In a darkened room, turn on the flashlight and shine it on the white screen. Note the color of the screen.

4. Lay the flashlight on the table beside and at an angle to the screen as shown.

5. Hold the sheet of yellow paper about 12 inches (30 cm) or more in front of the white paper. Then slowly move the yellow paper toward the screen until it is as close as the bulb end of the flashlight. As you move the yellow paper note the color of the screen.

6. Repeat step 5 using the sheet of red paper.

Results The screen looks white when the light is directed toward it but looks yellow when the light first hits the yellow paper and red when the light first hits the red paper.

Why? The yellow and red paper are colored because of pigments (natural substances that give color to a material). The light from the flashlight is basically white, so it has the rainbow colors (red, orange, yellow, green, blue, indigo, and violet). When white light hits a white object, such as the paper, the material absorbs very little light and reflects all the colored light. All the reflected colored light blended together produces white light, so the object looks white. The color you see depends on the colors reflected by the object that reach your eye. The pigments in the yellow paper absorb all the colors in white light except yellow. It reflects yellow light toward the screen, which reflects it to your eye. Thus, the screen appears to be yellow. The same is true for the red paper: it absorbs all the colors in white light except red, which it reflects.

Solutions to Exercises

1a. *Think!*

- The Sun gives off radiant energy.

- What is the name of the Sun's radiant energy?

Energy from the Sun is commonly called solar energy.

b. *Think!*

- Ultraviolet radiation comes from the Sun.

- Ultraviolet radiation causes skin to tan.

- If skin absorbs too much ultraviolet light, it can burn the skin or possibly cause skin cancer.

Ultraviolet radiation tans the skin and in excess could cause harm to the skin.

c. *Think!*

- A timer could be used to help limit the time in the sunlight.

- More clothing would protect the skin beneath it.

- Sunblock lotions can protect the skin by absorbing ultraviolet light, so the skin does not receive as much of the light.

The girl can protect her body from excessive UV rays by limiting her time in the sunlight, wearing protective clothing and sunglasses, and covering her skin with sunblock lotion.

2a. *Think!*

- Radiant energy from the Sun is called solar energy.

- Visible light is a form of solar energy. What is the source of white light?

The radiant energy source of white light is solar energy.

b. *Think!*

- White light is a mixture of all the colors of light in the visible spectrum.

- When white light hits an object, the color of the object is reflected.

- Which color making up white light is reflected by the flower?

The flower reflects red light, so it appears to be red.

12

Hot to Cold

Heat Transfer

What You Need to Know

Matter is made up of particles, such as atoms, molecules, and ions. The sum of all the energy of all the particles of an object is called **thermal energy** (also called internal energy).

It is commonly said that hot objects have more heat than cold objects, but technically the energy in the hot object is not heat; it is thermal energy. **Heat** is the energy that flows from a warm material to a cool material due to differences in temperature. An object is said to be heated when heat is added to it. An object that is heated has an increase in thermal energy as well as an increase in temperature. The reverse is true when an object is cooled.

Temperature is the measure of the average kinetic energy of the moving particles in a material; it is a measure of how hot or cold something is. But temperature is not a measure of the amount of thermal energy. For example, a bowl of soup and a cup of soup may have the same temperature, but there are more moving particles in the bowl of soup because there is more soup. Therefore, there is more kinetic energy and thermal energy in the bowl of soup than in the cup of soup.

When objects with different temperatures touch each other, the warmer object loses heat to the cooler object. Heat always flows from an object with more thermal energy to an object with less thermal energy. Heat does not always travel in the

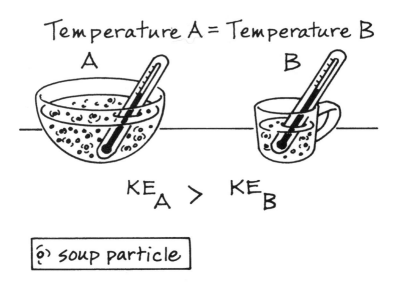

same manner. The three basic ways that heat is transferred are radiation, convection, and conduction.

Radiation is the method in which heat is transferred in the form of infrared radiation. **Convection** is the method in which heat is transferred by means of movement of heated **fluids** (liquid or gaseous materials that can move freely). **Conduction** is the method by which heat is transferred from one particle to another by collisions of the particles, also called **thermal conduction**. Heat is transferred faster by radiation than by convection or conduction. This is because radiant heat travels at the speed of light, which is 186,000 miles (300 million meters) per second. See chapter 11 for more information about heat transfer by radiation and chapter 13 for more information about heat transfer by convection.

In the process of conduction, heat is transferred through a substance, or from one substance to another, by the direct contact of particles. Because all matter is made of particles, conduction takes place in solids, liquids, and gases. For example, if a metal spoon is placed in a cup of hot chocolate, in time the handle of the spoon heats up, as does the air around the cup and spoon. This is because the faster-moving particles of hot chocolate collide with the slower-moving metal particles on the surface of the spoon's bowl. In these collisions, heat is transferred from the hot chocolate to the particles of the spoon. As heat is lost from the chocolate particles, their kinetic energy decreases; as heat is gained by the metal particles, their kinetic energy increases. The faster-moving metal particles in the spoon's bowl collide with the slower-moving neighboring particles in the spoon's handle. Thus, the heat from the hot chocolate is transferred from particle to particle through the spoon. In the process, the hot chocolate gets cooler and the spoon gets hotter. The same thing happens where the air particles touch the cup, hot chocolate, or spoon. Heat is transferred to the air particles. In time all the materials—cup, hot chocolate, and spoon—are the same temperature and there is no heat transfer.

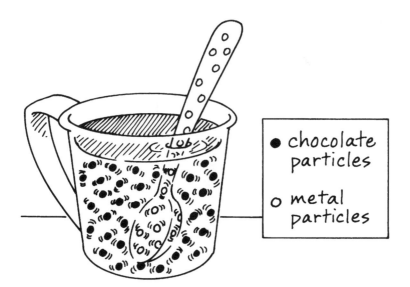

● chocolate particles

o metal particles

Some substances more easily transfer heat by conduction than other substances. These are called **conductors**. A conductor is called a **thermal conductor** when referring to its ability to conduct heat. Metals are good conductors. Substances that are poor conductors are called **insulators**. An insulator is called a **thermal insulator** when referring to its inability to conduct heat. Glass, wood, and trapped air, such as between the feathers of a bird, are good insulators.

Exercises

1. The water in figures A and B is the same temperature. Which figure, A or B, has more thermal energy?

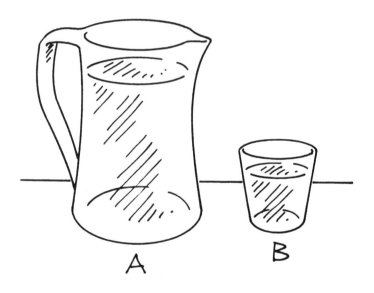

2. In the figure, two metal blocks of different temperatures are touching. Which arrow choice, A, B, or C, indicates the direction that heat is transferred between the blocks?

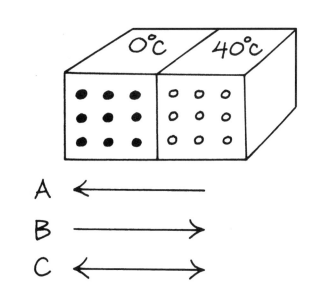

Activity: LOSER

Purpose   To demonstrate heat transfer by conduction.

Materials   metal cookie sheet
18-inch (45-cm) piece of string

Procedure

1. Place the cookie sheet on a table.

2. Press your right hand against the surface and near one end of the cookie sheet. Using your other hand, stretch the string around the hand that is on the cookie sheet to outline it.

3. With the string in place, continue to press your hand against the cookie sheet for 30 or more seconds. Measure the time in seconds by counting one thousand and one, one thousand and two, one thousand and three, and so on, to one thousand and thirty.

4. Before lifting your hand from the cookie sheet, place the fingers on your left hand against its surface at the opposite end. Note how warm or cool the cookie sheet feels.

5. Then lift your right hand and touch your left hand to the area of the cookie sheet within the string outline that was covered by your right hand. Note how warm or cool the area feels.

Results The cookie sheet feels warmer in the area within the string outline.

Why? Conduction is the process by which heat is transferred between objects in contact with each other. The heat moves from the warmer object to the cooler one. The cookie sheet is at room temperature and your body temperature is about 98.6° F (37°C), which is generally much warmer than room temperature. When you touch your hand to the cookie sheet, heat from your hand moves to the cookie sheet because of conduction. The thermal energy of the skin touching the cookie sheet decreases and the thermal energy of the cookie sheet increases. Thus, the cookie sheet's temperature within the string outline increases. Outside the string, the temperature of the cookie sheet does not increase, so it feels cooler. The sensation of coolness or warmness depends on how much heat leaves or enters your skin. The more heat leaving the skin, the cooler the object feels.

Solutions to Exercises

1. *Think!*

- Thermal energy is the total of all the energy of all the particles of a substance.

- At the same temperature, the average kinetic energy of the particles of water in the pitcher and glass is the same.

- As the number of particles increases, the thermal energy increases.

- Which figure, A or B, has more particles?

Figure A has more particles and therefore more thermal energy.

2. *Think!*

- Heat is the transfer of thermal energy from warmer objects to cooler objects.

- Which arrow shows the direction from the warmer block to the cooler block?

Arrow A shows the direction of heat transfer from the warmer block to the cooler block of metal.

13

Currents

Transfer by Convection

What You Need to Know

When a fluid (gas or liquid) is heated, its **volume** (amount of space an object takes up) increases because its particles have more energy and they begin to move faster and farther apart. Thus, a cold fluid would have a smaller volume than an equal mass of the same fluid at a higher temperature. When the volume of a material increases but the mass stays the same, the density (measure of the mass per volume) of the material decreases. So the number of particles remains the same, but the particles are spread out more.

If you compared equal number of particles of a warm and a cold fluid, the warm sample would have a lower density. For example, both balloons in the figure have 12 gas particles, but the balloon with warm gas has expanded, so the gas particles are more spread out. The balloon with warm gas has 12 particles in a larger volume than the cold gas. So the warm gas balloon has a lower density than that of the cold gas balloon.

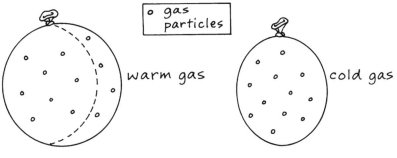

The difference in the density of fluids causes warmer, less dense fluids to rise and colder, denser fluids to sink. The transfer of heat by the movement of heated fluid particles is called convection, and the up-and-down movement of fluid particles due to differences in density as a result of differences in temperature is called a **convection current**. A common example of heat transfer by convection is the movement of air in a room. The warm, less dense air rises toward the ceiling and the cold, denser air sinks toward the floor. The best way to warm a room in the winter is to heat the air near the floor. The heated air will rise to the ceiling. When this warm air cools, it will sink back to the floor; as a result, convection currents will be formed, moving warm air around the room.

Convection currents are found in Earth's atmosphere and in the oceans. In the atmosphere, air near Earth's surface is warmed and rises, and cool air sinks, forming convection currents. These currents transfer heat throughout Earth's atmosphere. Similar movements of water in the oceans produce ocean currents that transfer heat from one area to another.

Exercises

1. Study the figure and determine which area, A, B, or C, will have a warmer temperature.

2. Which figure, A, B, or C, does not show motion due to convection currents?

A

B

C

Activity: STREAMERS

Purpose   To demonstrate convection currents due to temperature differences.

Materials   masking tape
pen
four 9-ounce (270-ml) transparent plastic cups
warm and cold tap water
2 ice cubes
drinking straw
red food coloring
adult helper

Procedure

1. Use the tape and pen to label two cups "Warm" and the two remaining cups "Cold."

2. Fill one of the cold cups three-fourths full with cold tap water. Add the ice to this cup.

3. Stir the icy water several times with the straw. Remove and discard the ice, then pour about half of the water into the other cold cup.

4. Add 10 drops of red food coloring to one of the cups of cold water. Stir with the straw.

5. Ask an adult to fill the warm cups half full with warm tap water. Add 10 drops of food coloring to one of the cups of warm water. Stir with the straw.

6. Set the cup of uncolored warm water on a table and sit so that you are eye level with the cup.

7. Stand the straw in the colored cold water. Keep the water in the straw by placing your finger over the open end.

8. Place the straw in the cup of uncolored warm water. Slightly raise your finger from the end of the straw to

allow the colored cold water to leave the straw. Observe the movement of the colored water.

9. Remove the straw from the water and observe the contents of the cup periodically for about 5 minutes.

10. Repeat steps 6 through 9, but use uncolored cold water in step 6 and colored warm water in step 7.

Results The colored cold water flows out of the straw and settles on the bottom of the cup of warm water. The colored warm water flows out of the straw and rises to the surface of the cold water. The colored warm water mixes with the cold water as it rises, thus coloring the cold water. But a darker layer of colored water forms on the surface of the cold water.

Why? Convection is the transfer of heat by moving fluid, such as water, due to differences in temperature. Warm-water molecules have more energy and move around faster than less energetic cold-water molecules. The speedy warm-water molecules tend to move away from each other. So warm water, with its molecules spaced farther apart, is less dense than cold water. When the colored cold water was released at the bottom of a cup filled with warm water, the denser cold water sank to the bottom of the cup. When the colored warm water was released at the bottom of the cup filled with cold water, the warm water, which was less dense than the cold water, rose to the surface. During its movement to the surface, there was some mixing of the colored warm water with the uncolored cold water. But most of it rose to the surface, forming a dark layer there. In the cup as in nature, cold surface water sinks as the warmer water rises and takes its place. This rising of warm water and sinking of cold water produces convection currents.

Solutions to Exercises

1. *Think!*

   - The heater warms the air near the floor.

   - Warm air is less dense and is lighter than cold air. So the warm air rises to the ceiling.

   - Which area is nearest the ceiling, A, B, or C?

   Area C is nearest the ceiling, so it is the warmest area.

2. *Think!*

   - Convection currents are the up-and-down movement of particles due to differences in fluid density as a result of temperature differences.

   - Figure A has motion of a fluid, water, but there is no indication of a temperature difference.

   - Figure B shows motion due to heated air rising and hitting the spiral.

   - Figure C shows a hot air balloon filled by heated air.

- The heated air inside the balloon is less dense than the colder air surrounding the balloon, so the balloon rises.

- Which figure, A, B, or C, does not show motion due to convection currents?

Figure A does not show motion due to convection currents.

14

Warm Up!

Infrared Radiation

What You Need to Know

Solar energy is the radiation emitted by the Sun and contains all the types of radiation in the electromagnetic spectrum. But most of the solar radiation reaching Earth's atmosphere is **thermal radiation** (radiation emitted by an object as a result of its temperature), which is made up of ultraviolet radiation, visible light, and infrared radiation (invisible radiation that is felt as heat). Radiation is absorbed, reflected, and passes through the atmosphere.

Any material that absorbs or reflects a specific type of radiation without allowing any to pass through is said to be **opaque** (blocks the passage of radiation) to that type of radiation. For example, your body is opaque to visible light. A material that allows a specific type of radiation to pass through it without a change in the direction of the radiation is said to be **transparent** (doesn't block the passage of radiation) to that type of radiation. Clear glass is transparent to visible light. If the radiation passing through a material is **diffused** (spread in different directions), the material is said to be **translucent** to that type of radiation. Frosted glass is translucent to visible light.

A material might be transparent to one form of radiation and opaque to another. For example, clear glass is transparent to visible light but opaque to infrared radiation. Infrared radiation is absorbed by the glass, but visible light passes through. Since light passes directly through the glass, you can clearly

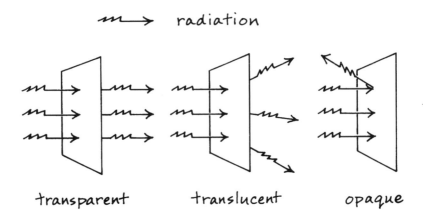

see objects through the glass. The lighter and shinier the object, the more it reflects radiation. Dark colored objects absorb more radiation than light colored objects.

Radiation that is absorbed causes the temperature of the absorbing material to increase. For example, visible light from the Sun passing through the glass in a window is absorbed by different materials inside the room. Dark-colored materials with dull, soft, or rough surfaces absorb more light than light-colored, shiny, hard surfaces. The absorbed light causes the particles in these materials to move faster, thus increasing their kinetic energy. As the kinetic energy of particles increases, the thermal energy of a material increases, and the material gets hotter. Heat from hot materials is transferred to cooler materials by conduction, convection, or radiation (emission of infrared radiation). The glass in the window is opaque to the infrared radiation produced inside the room, but the glass is warmed by the infrared radiation it absorbs. Because materials such as air and curtains touch the warmed glass, some of the heat from the glass is transferred to the outside and some is returned to the room by conduction.

All objects are constantly emitting or receiving infrared radiation. The higher the temperature of an object with respect to its surroundings, the faster it emits infrared radiation. The lower the temperature of an object with respect to its surroundings, the faster it absorbs infrared radiation. Thus, hot bodies tend to emit infrared radiation and cold bodies tend to absorb it.

If you sit near a campfire, you are warmed mainly by heat energy transferred from the fire by radiation. This is because the heat transferred by convection currents rises instead of moving toward you. Since air is a very poor conductor of heat, you receive little to no warmth due to conduction. While visible light that is absorbed is converted to heat energy, the fire produces very little visible light for your body to absorb. Campfires are generally not hot enough to produce UV radiation. So infrared radiation provides most of the warmth you receive from a campfire.

Exercises

1. Study the figure on page 108 and determine which symbol, A or B, represents infrared radiation.

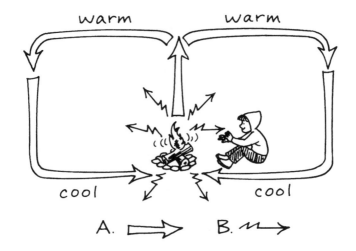

2. Which of the figures, A, B, or C, shows the marshmallow being heated by infrared radiation?

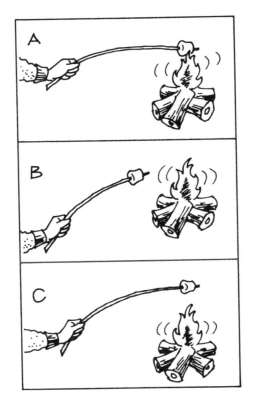

Activity: STRAIGHT THROUGH

Purpose To compare the effect of materials on the transfer of infrared radiation.

Materials 6-by-6-inch (15-by-15-cm) piece of white plastic garbage bag

6-by-6-inch (15-by-15-cm) piece of white poster board

desk lamp

Procedure

1. Turn the lamp on and adjust it so that the light shines down.

2. Hold one hand, palm side up, about 4 inches (10 cm) below the bulb of the lamp for 5 seconds. Measure the time in seconds by counting one thousand and one, one thousand and two, and so on. Note how warm or cool your hand feels while under the light. *Caution: Do not hold your hand closer than 4 inches (10 cm) below the bulb.* Remove your hand if your skin starts to feel uncomfortably warm.

3. Remove your hand from under the light and allow it to cool for 5 seconds. Then cover your palm with the square of white plastic and repeat step 2.

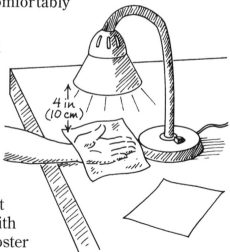

4. Repeat step 2, but cover your hand with the square of white poster board.

Results The skin of your hand feels warmest without a covering, medium warm with the plastic covering, and coolest with the poster board covering.

Why? The lamp gives off infrared radiation, which is absorbed by your skin, causing your skin to feel warm. The poster board blocks infrared radiation; the plastic only blocks some of it. This is why your hand feels warmest with no covering, medium warm when covered with the plastic, and coolest when covered with the poster board.

Solutions to Exercises

1. *Think!*

   • Heat moves by convection when the heated air above a fire rises and cool air takes its place. Which arrow represents convection? A

   • Heat moves away from a fire in all directions by radiation in the form of infrared radiation.

   • Of the two choices of heat transfer shown by arrows in the figure, which arrow represents infrared radiation?

   In the figure, arrow B represents heat transfer by infrared radiation.

2. *Think!*

   • In figure A, the marshmallow is heated by conduction because it touches the hot flames.

   • In figure C, the marshmallow is heated by the hot air rising from the fire. Thus, it is heated by convection.

- The marshmallow in figure B is not above the fire and is not touching the flame. Thus, it is being heated by the heat transfer called radiation, and the type of radiation being transferred is infrared radiation.

Figure B shows heat being transferred to the marshmallow by infrared radiation.

15

Changes

How Thermal Energy
Is Measured

What You Need to Know

Thermal energy is the total energy of a material (see chapter 12 for more about thermal energy), and heat is the transfer of thermal energy from one object to another. Temperature is a measure of the average kinetic energy of all the particles making up an object. When heat is added to an object, there is an increase in the average kinetic energy of the particles, so there is a rise in temperature of the object. Likewise, when heat is lost by an object, the average kinetic energy of its particles decreases and the temperature of the object decreases. Temperature, therefore, is a measure of how hot or cold an object is. If you dip your finger into a bowl of warm water, then touch your finger to an ice cube, you can determine that one object has a higher temperature than the other. But while your body is sensitive to differences in hotness and coldness of an object, it cannot be used to determine specific degrees of temperature.

An instrument called a **thermometer** is used to measure temperature. Many types of thermometers are used today. One type has a small-diameter tube that opens into a liquid-filled bulb. At one time the liquid in most thermometers was mercury. But it is now known that mercury is **toxic** (poisonous), so other liquids are being used. Today a safe vegetable oil–type liquid and dye mixture is being used in some thermometers. When the liquid in the bulb is heated, its particles move faster and farther apart. The heated liquid expands, rising in the tube. The opposite happens when the liquid is cooled. The particles move more slowly and get closer together, and the liquid's height in the tube drops. In order to measure changes in the liquid, a scale is printed along the tube.

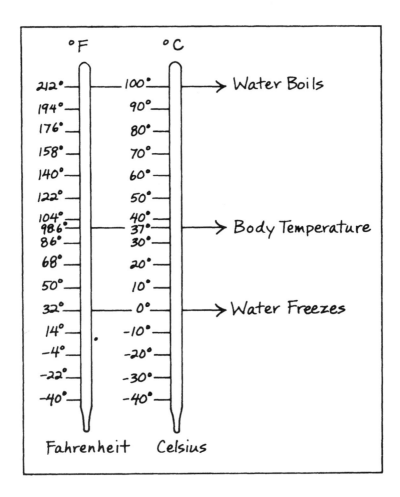

The two commonly used scales are Fahrenheit and Celsius. The **Fahrenheit scale** is named after the German scientist Daniel Gabriel Fahrenheit (1686–1736). The unit of temperature on the Fahrenheit scale is the degree Fahrenheit, °F.

The **Celsius scale** is named after the Swedish scientist Anders Celsius (1701–1744). The unit of temperature on the Celsius scale is the degree Celsius, °C. These scales have the same two reference points—the freezing and boiling points of water—but differ in the values given to each. On the Fahrenheit scale, water freezes at 32°F and boils at 212°F at sea level. On the Celsius scale, which is used in most scientific work, water freezes at 0°C and boils at 100°C at sea level.

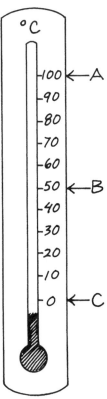

Exercises

Use the diagram of the thermometer shown here and the thermometer diagram on page 114 to answer the following:

1. Which temperature reading, A, B, or C, is the temperature of boiling water?

2. For the temperature reading A on the Celsius scale in the diagram, what is the same temperature on a Fahrenheit scale?

Activity: FEELINGS

Purpose To demonstrate how accurate touch is in measuring temperature.

Materials 2 spoons of equal size—1 metal, 1 plastic

Procedure

1. Place both spoons on a table for 5 minutes or more.

2. Hold the bottom of the metal spoon's bowl against your cheek. Note how hot or cold the spoon feels.

3. Repeat step 2 using the plastic spoon.

Results The metal spoon feels colder than the plastic spoon.

Why? The temperatures of the metal and plastic spoons are the same. The metal spoon is a better conductor of heat than the plastic spoon. This means that heat flows more easily through the metal than through the plastic. When you touch the spoons, more heat is transferred from your skin to the metal spoon than to the plastic spoon. The metal spoon feels colder because the nerves in your skin send messages to your brain that heat is being lost. Thus, you are aware of the transfer of heat rather than the actual temperature of the spoons.

Solutions to Exercises

1. *Think!*

- The diagram represents a thermometer with a Celsius scale.

- On the Celsius scale, what is the temperature of boiling water? 100°C

Temperature reading A shows the temperature of boiling water.

2. *Think!*

- Reading A on the Celsius scale in the diagram is 100°C, the temperature for boiling water.

- What is the temperature for boiling water on the Fahrenheit scale?

For a temperature of 100°C, the same temperature on a Fahrenheit scale is 212°F.

16

Opposite

Electric Charges

What You Need to Know

A **charge (electric charge)** is the property of particles within atoms that causes an electric force between the particles. Electric charges occur in nature in two forms, and the American scientist and statesman Benjamin Franklin (1706–1783) named them positive and negative. **Electricity** is a form of energy. There are two kinds of electricity: static electricity and current electricity. **Static electricity** is due to the presence of **static charges** (buildup of stationary charges), and **current electricity** is due to moving charges. The energy associated with electricity is called **electric energy. Potential electric energy** is due to the attractive or repulsive forces between electrical charges.

When two like charges (positive and positive or negative and negative) are near each other, they **repel** (push apart) each other. But when two unlike charges (positive and negative) are near each other, they attract (pull together) each other. This is called the **law of electric charges**. Potential energy (PE) increases when objects that repel each other are pushed together and when objects that attract each other are pulled apart. So, as the distance varies between electrical charges, so do their potential electrical energies.

An atom is made up of a small, dense center called the nucleus. The basic particles in the nucleus are protons and neutrons. Nuclear particles, whether protons or neutrons, are known collectively as **nucleons**. Surrounding the nucleus are rapidly moving particles called electrons (e'). Protons and electrons have electrical charges. Protons have a positive charge, which is indicated by a plus sign (+), and electrons have a negative charge, which is indicated by a negative sign (–). Neutrons have no charge, so they are neutral, which is indicated by a combination of a positive and a negative sign (±).

An atom is **neutral** if it has a balanced number of positive and negative charges, which means is has an equal number of protons and electrons. Thus, even though an atom contains charged particles, it is electrically neutral because the charges cancel each other out. Atoms can become charged by either losing or gaining electrons. This happens because electrons, unlike protons, are free to move. If an atom loses an electron, it has more positive charges (protons) than negative charges (electrons), so it becomes positively charged. If an atom gains an electron, it has more negative charges (electrons) than positive charges (protons), so it becomes negatively charged.

Two methods by which neutral materials are charged are friction and conduction. **Charging by friction** is the process of charging two neutral materials as a result of physical contact between them. One of the materials tends to lose electrons more than the other, so the loss of electrons results in it becoming positively charged, and the gain of electrons by the other material results in it becoming negatively charged. This occurs when you walk across a carpet. A static charge forms when your shoes rub electrons from the carpet. These electrons spread across your body, so your body becomes negatively charged. The carpet has lost electrons and becomes positively charged. **Charging by conduction** is the method of electrically charging a neutral object by touching it with a charged object.

The repulsion or attraction of charged particles occurs even if they are not touching each other. This is because there is an electric field, which is the region around a charged parti-

cle in which a force acts on an electric charge brought into
the region. For the positive and negative charges in the figure, **lines of force** are drawn to indicate the presence of the
electric field. When two charged particles come near each
other, the direction of the lines of force is altered. If the two
charges are not alike, the lines of force curve between the
charges form a bridge. If the two charges are alike, the lines
of force between the charges are repelled, so they curve
away from both charges.

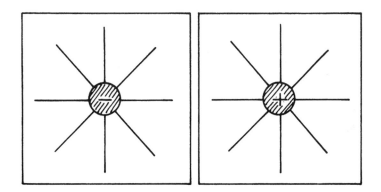

Exercises

1. Which balloon, A or B, is charged?

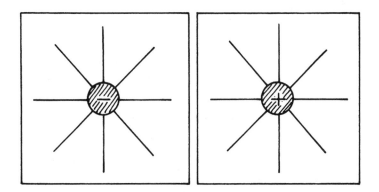

Study the figures to answer the following:

2. Which figure, A or B, represents the lines of force between two like charges?

3. Which figure, A or B, represents the lines of force between two unlike charges?

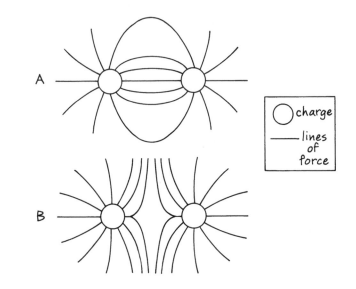

Activity: SEPARATOR

Purpose　To demonstrate the force of repulsion between materials due to static electricity.

Materials　transparent tape

Procedure

1. Tear off a strip of tape about 8 inches (20 cm) long from the roll of tape.

2. Stick one end of the strip of tape to the edge of a table so that most of the tape hangs down from the table's edge.

3. Tear off a second 8-inch (20 cm) piece of tape from the tape roll.

4. Hold one edge of the second strip of tape near but not touching the tape hanging from the table. Observe the immediate position of the two hanging strips of tape.

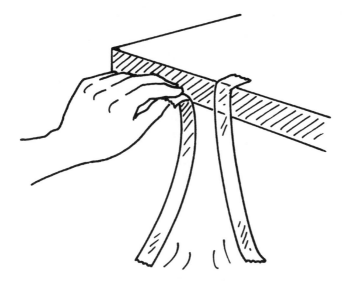

Results The pieces of tape immediately move apart when placed near one another.

Why? When you pull the tape off the roll, you are pulling some atoms in the tape apart, which is an example of charging by friction. As the sticky and unsticky sides of the tape separate, electrons are either lost or gained by the strip. Assume the strip gains electrons and is negatively charged. There is a buildup of negative charges on the tape. Since the two strips have like charges and like charges repel one another, the strips move apart.

The repulsion of the strips is caused by static electricity. In time the static charge is lost. **Static discharge** is the loss of static electricity. It occurs when electrons on the strips of tape are picked up by air molecules or more likely water molecules in the air that transfer the electrons to other materials they touch, and so on. Water molecules are **polarized** (have a positive end and a negative end). The positive end attracts and holds the electrons to carry them off. This explains why there is little static electricity when the **humidity** (measure of the amount of water vapor in air) is high.

The static discharge from the tape strips was slow and quiet, but sometimes static discharge is very rapid and noisy, such as **lightning** (visible static discharge between clouds or a cloud and Earth) accompanied by **thunder** (loud sound produced by the expansion of air that has been heated by lightning).

Solutions to Exercises

1. *Think!*

- There are two types of charges, positive (+) and negative (–).

- A material with an unequal number of positive and negative charges is said to be charged.

- Balloon A has four positive and four negative charges. Balloon B has four positive and seven negative charges.

- Which figure, A or B, has an unequal number of positive and negative charges?

Figure B is charged due to an unequal number of positive and negative charges.

2. *Think!*

- When two like charges are near each other, the lines of force between them are repelled, so they bend away from the other charges.

- Which figure, A or B, shows lines of force from each charge bending away from the facing charge?

Figure B represents the presence of two like charges.

3. *Think!*

- When two unlike charges are near each other, the lines of force between them are attracted, so they form a bridge.

- Which figure, A or B, shows the lines of force between the charges bending from one charge to the other?

Figure A represents the presence of two unlike charges.

17

Stop and Go

Electricity

What You Need to Know

Electricity results from the presence of stationary or moving charges. The energy associated with electricity is called electrical energy. There are two kinds of electricity: static electricity and current electricity. Static electricity is due to the buildup of stationary electric charges. Current electricity is due to the motion of **free electrons** (electrons in some solids, particularly metals, that are not tightly bound to a single atom and are relatively free to move through the solid).

Electrical charges do not easily build up on some materials, such as metals. Instead, the charges are easily conducted through by these materials. Thus, they are called **electric conductors**. Materials that transfer electricity easily also transfer heat easily; thus, the term conductor indicates a material that is an electrical conductor and a thermal conductor. Conductors have a high **concentration** (measure of the amount of substance in an area) of free electrons. Metals are good conductors, especially silver, copper, and aluminum. Earth is also a good conductor.

Conduction is the process of transferring electric energy or heat from one particle to another by collisions of the particles. **Electric conduction** is the transfer of electric energy associated with current electricity through a conductor due to the movement of free electrons in the material.

Materials that are poor conductors of heat and electricity are called insulators. These materials have a low concentration of free electrons. A material is called an **electric insulator** with reference to its ability to restrict the movement of charges through it. Good insulators include rubber, glass, wood, plastic, and air. Since charges do not easily move through an insulator, unlike a conductor, charges more easily collect on an insulator. For example, if you rub a rubber balloon on your hair, the balloon rubs electrons from your hair. These electrons collect on the balloon, resulting in the balloon having a negative static charge. Your hair is left with a positive static charge. The strands of your hair repel each other because they have like charges. If you hold the negatively charged balloon near but not touching your charged hair, strands of hair move toward the balloon because of the attraction between unlike charges. This repulsion and attraction between charged objects is an example of static electricity. The static charge on your hair and the balloon is eventually lost through static discharge.

A neutral material can be polarized (have positive and negative ends due to a separation of positive and negative charges) because of the nearness of a charged object. This is called **electrostatic induction**. In this method, holding a charged object near but not touching a neutral object results in a rearrangement of the electric charges in the neutral object. For example, if the negatively charged balloon is brought near a ceiling, the electrons in the region of the ceiling nearest to the charged balloon are repelled, leaving this region of the ceiling positively charged. This positive surface is attracted to the negatively charged balloon. If the static electricity is strong enough to overcome the downward force of gravity, the balloon will stick to the ceiling.

The study of the cause, nature, behavior, and uses of static electricity is called **electrostatics**. Static electricity has many uses—for example, electrostatic copying machines make duplicates of printed material by attracting negatively charged particles of powdered ink to positively charged paper. Another use of static electricity is in some air cleaners, which pull air from a room into the device and positively charge the dust, smoke, pollen, and any other particles in the air. Collector plates with a negative charge then attract the positive particles, thereby cleaning the air.

Exercises

Study figures A, B, and C to answer the following:

1. Which figure represents a neutral material?

2. Which figure has a static charge?

3. Which figure represents a polarized material?

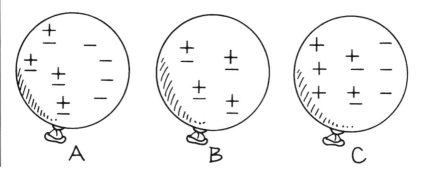

Activity: ATTRACTIVE

Purpose   To demonstrate static electricity.

Materials   sheet of copy paper
salt shaker with salt
9-inch (22.5-cm) round balloon
wool scarf

Procedure

1. Lay the paper on a table.

2. Sprinkle a thin layer of salt over the center of the paper.

3. Inflate the balloon to about the size of a grapefruit. Tie the balloon.

4. Charge the balloon by rubbing it back and forth on the scarf five or more times.

5. Hold the balloon near but not touching the salt.

Results The particles of salt jump up and stick to the balloon.

Why? Rubbing the balloon on the scarf results in electrons moving from the scarf to the balloon. When the rubbing stops and the balloon and scarf are separated, the electric charges stop moving. The electric charges on each material remain stationary, so each has a static charge. The balloon has a negative charge. When you hold it near the salt particles, it causes the salt to be polarized by electrostatic induction. The salt still has a balance of positive and negative charges, but these charges have separated because of the charged balloon. The electrons on the side of the salt facing the negatively charged balloon are repelled, leaving a buildup of positive charges on that side. The attraction between this positive surface and the negatively charged balloon is great enough to lift the salt and stick it to the balloon.

Solutions to Exercises

1. *Think!*

- A neutral material has a balanced number of positive and negative charges.
- Which figure has the same number of positive and negative charges?

Figures B and C represent a material that is neutral.

2. *Think!*

- A material with a static charge has more of one kind of charge than the other.
- Which figure has an unbalanced number of charges?

Figure A represents a material with a static charge.

3. *Think!*

- A material is polarized when it has an equal number of positive and negative charges, but some of these charges are separated.

- Which figure has an equal number of positive and negative charges with more positive charges on one side and more negative charges on the other side?

Figure C represents a polarized material.

18

Pushers

Batteries

What You Need to Know

Current electricity is the flow of electric charges due to the motion of free electrons in a conductor. A wall light switch is connected to the bulb in a ceiling lamp by conducting wire. When you turn on the switch, the lamp seems to instantly glow. Free electrons do not flow through the wire like water flows through a pipe. Instead, due to the electric field around each free electron, the motion of electrons at one end of a conductor causes an almost instantaneous movement of all the free electrons. For example, when an electron in a conductor moves, it travels into the force field of a neighboring electron. The repulsion between the two electrons causes the neighboring electron to move forward. Since there is a force field around all the electrons, as soon as one free electron moves forward, the repulsive forces between all the electrons instantaneously cause them to move. While the forward speed of the free electrons is about 0.0003 feet (0.00009 m) per second, the speed of the transfer of electrical energy is about 30 million times as fast. **Current (I)** is a term used for current electricity, which is the measure of the amount of electric charge per second that is moving through a conductor.

An **electric cell** is a device that changes chemical energy into electrical energy. Two or more cells combined make up a **battery**. But battery is a common name for some single electric cells, such as a flashlight battery. So in this book the term *battery* is used for single-celled flashlight batteries. The energy in flashlight batteries, or any battery with multiple cells, cannot be used until the battery's two **terminals** (points at which connections are made to an electrical device) are connected by a conductor, such as a metal wire. Cells have two kinds of terminals: a **positive terminal** (terminal with a positive charge) and a **negative terminal** (terminal with a negative charge).

An electric cell contains **electrodes** (conductors in a cell that collect or give up electrons) and an **electrolyte** (mixture of chemicals that produces a chemical reaction in which electric charges are released). The change of chemical energy into electrical energy in a cell is due to a chemical reaction taking place between the electrodes and the electrolyte, resulting in one electrode becoming positively charged and the other negatively charged. In common flashlight cells, such as those used in the Activity section of this chapter, the elements zinc and carbon act as the electrodes. The zinc is the outer can of the cell, forming the negative terminal. Inside the zinc can is a dry chemical paste with the carbon rod in the center. The carbon rod is connected to the positive terminal. When the terminals are connected by a conductor, chemical reactions in the battery result in electrons leaving the negative terminal and entering the positive terminal of the battery. This type of cell is called a **dry cell** because the electrolyte is a chemical paste instead of a liquid as in **wet cells**, such as car batteries.

The path through which electric charges move is called an **electric circuit**. The unit used to measure current is the **ampere (A)** (amp, for short). One amp (1 A) is equal to 6.25×10^{18} electric charges per second. When a metal wire is connected to a battery, the free electrons in the wire start to move from the negative terminal to the positive terminal. This drift of electrons is called the electric current. As the electrons move, they bump into the atoms in the wire and are slowed down. This braking or slowing-down effect is called **resistance (R)** (opposition of the flow of electric current) of the conductor. The diameter of a wire affects its resistance. The smaller the diameter, the greater its resistance. The length of the wire also affects resistance. The longer the wire, the greater its resistance.

Volt (V) is a unit used to measure the potential energy per charge in a battery. The potential energy of a battery varies with the difference in the volts between the terminals. This difference is called **potential difference** or **voltage**, and it is a measure of the amount of push on electric charges. The greater the potential difference, the greater the potential energy; thus, the greater the push on electrons in a circuit. As the potential difference increases, the amount of current that flows through a circuit increases. A 1.5-V battery tells you that the potential difference between the terminals is 1.5 volts. A 6-V battery has four times as much potential difference as a 1.5-V battery. When connected to electric circuits, the 6-V battery gives electric charges four times as much push as the 1.5-V battery. In a circuit with the same resistance, a battery with a higher voltage will produce more current than one with a lower voltage.

Exercises

1. Which figure of a ball dropping, A or B, correctly represents the potential energy difference between a 6-V and a 12-V battery?

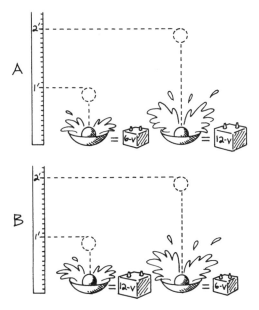

2. Which figure, A or B, correctly represents the effect that wire length has on the resistance of current flow?

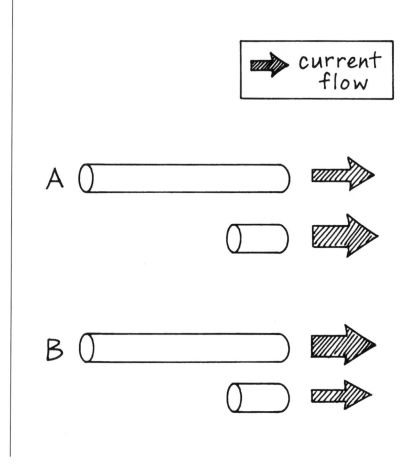

Activity: **BRIGHTER**

Purpose   To compare the electric energy of batteries with different voltage amounts.

Materials 2-by-18-inch (5-by-45-cm) piece of aluminum foil
1-inch (2.5-cm) -wide masking tape
scissors
screw-base flashlight bulb
clothespin
2 size D (1.5-V) dry-cell batteries

Procedure

Caution: Use only 1.5-V batteries. Do not use more than two batteries. More than two batteries could produce a dangerous amount of current.

1. Prepare an aluminum foil strip by placing an 18-inch (45-cm) piece of masking tape down on the piece of aluminum foil.

2. Cut along the edges of the tape. Then fold the strip in half with the tape sides together. Crease the fold.

3. Tightly wrap one end of the foil strip around the threaded metal base of the flashlight bulb. Secure with the clothespin.

4. Stand the flat, negative terminal of one of the batteries on the free end of the foil strip so that it's touching the foil side.

5. Squeeze the clothespin tightly against the base of the bulb while pressing the bulb's metal bottom against the raised, positive terminal of the battery. Note the degree of brightness from the bulb.

foil strip

1.5 V

6. Remove the bulb from the top of the battery. Then stand a second battery on top of the first one. The positive terminal of one battery must touch the negative terminal of the other battery.

7. Using the combined batteries, repeat step 5.

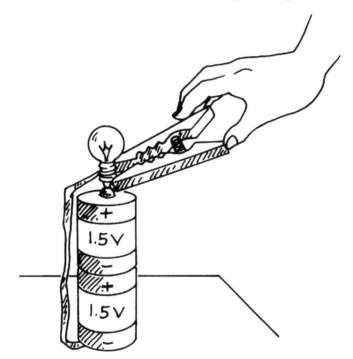

Results The bulb glows more brightly when you use the column of two batteries.

Why? The combination of the flashlight batteries, with the positive end of one touching the negative end of the other, creates one battery with one positive terminal and one negative terminal. The voltage of each battery is added together, so the new battery is 3 V. A 3-V battery has twice as much potential difference as a 1.5-V battery. When connected to the electric circuits, the combined batteries with 3 V give the electrical charges in the circuit twice as much push as the

1.5-V battery. So more current (charges per second) flows through the bulb, causing the **filament** (small-diameter wire usually made of tungsten) to get hot. The hotter the filament in the bulb, the brighter the light it emits. Flashlight bulbs are examples of **incandescent lamps**, which are light bulbs that produce light by heating a filament to a high temperature.

Solutions to Exercises

1. *Think!*

   - The potential energy of two balls dropped from different heights is compared to batteries with different voltages.

   - The higher the ball, the greater its potential energy.

   - The voltage of a battery indicates the potential difference between the battery terminals.

   - The greater the potential difference, the greater the potential energy stored in the battery.

   - Which figure matches the ball with low potential energy with the 6-V battery and the ball with greater potential energy with the 12-V battery?

   Figure A represents the potential energy difference between the two batteries.

2. *Think!*

   - The wires are the same diameter but different lengths.

   - A longer wire has more resistance to current flow because there are more atoms for the free electrons to bump into and slow them down.

   Figure A represents an increase in the resistance to current flow as the wire length increases.

19

Stick to It!

Magnetic Potential Energy

What You Need to Know

Magnets are objects made of magnetic material that produce a magnetic field (region around a magnet where its magnetic force affects other magnetic material). **Magnetic material** is attracted to a magnet and is used to make magnets. **Magnetic force** is the force of attraction (pulling together) or repulsion (pushing apart) between two magnets, or the force of attraction between a magnet and a magnetic material. For example, a magnet can be used to pick up metal paper clips because they are made of magnetic material. The force of attraction between the metal paper clips and the magnet holds the clips to the magnet.

Magnetism describes all effects of a magnetic field, including magnetic potential energy. Potential energy is the ability of an object to do work because of its position. The energy of an object that has the ability to do work because of its position in a magnetic field is called magnetic potential energy. Objects move in the direction that reduces their magnetic potential energy. For example, a paper clip held near but not touching a magnet has magnetic potential energy. When released, the paper clip will move toward the magnet, which reduces its magnetic potential energy.

All magnets, no matter the shape or size, have two regions where their magnetic force is strongest. These regions are called **magnetic poles**. One pole is called the north pole and the other the south pole. The **law of magnetic poles** states that like poles of a magnet (north and north or south and south) repel each other and unlike poles of a magnet (north and south) attract each other.

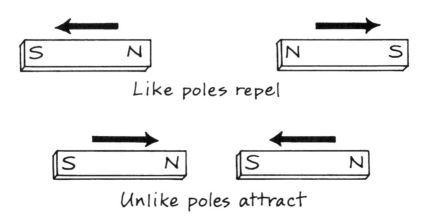

Like poles repel

Unlike poles attract

The most common magnetic materials are iron and iron **alloys** (material made by blending two or more elements, at least one being a metal). Steel is a magnetic alloy made of iron and carbon. Although all magnets are made of magnetic material, all magnetic materials are not magnets. This means the magnetic material in a magnet is **magnetized** (caused to have a magnetic field). But if the magnetic material is not a magnet, it is **unmagnetized** (doesn't have a magnetic field). Magnetism is caused by spinning electrons. Electrons spin about their axis as they move around the nucleus of an atom. This spin produces a magnetic field around the electrons. All electrons are like tiny magnets with north and south poles. But all electrons do not spin in the same direction; most are paired with a partner that spins in the opposite direction. Thus, their magnetic fields oppose each other and are canceled out. In **nonmagnetic materials**, the electrons in the atoms are all paired.

In atoms of magnetic materials, some electrons are not paired, which gives the atom as a whole a magnetic field. A group of these atoms with a single magnetic field around them forms a **magnetic domain**. Each magnetic domain acts like a microscopic magnet within a magnetic material. When a magnetic material is magnetized, most of its domains line up in the same direction. The combined fields of these domains produce the magnetic field around the object commonly called a magnet. The domains of unmagnetized magnetic materials are not lined up; instead, they point in many different directions, which causes their fields to cancel each other out, much like some positive and negative charges are canceled out when added together.

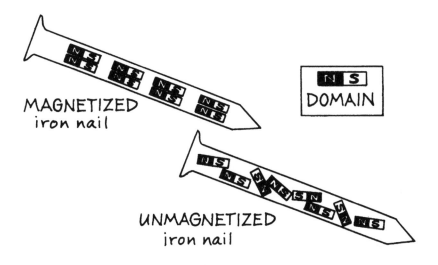

Exercises

1. Which figure, A or B, represents electrons found in magnetic material?

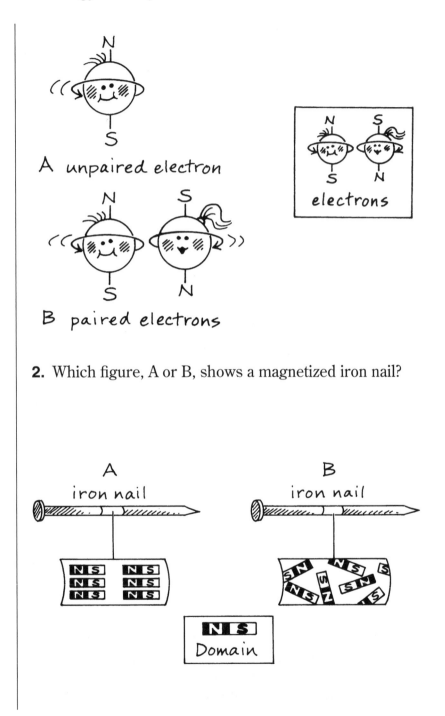

A unpaired electron

electrons

B paired electrons

2. Which figure, A or B, shows a magnetized iron nail?

A
iron nail

B
iron nail

Domain

Activity: STRONGER

Purpose   To demonstrate the effect of magnetic potential energy.

Materials   12-inch (30-cm) piece of string
paper clip
transparent tape
5 or more books
bar magnet
scissors

Procedure

1. Tie the string to the paper clip.

2. Tape the free end of the string to a table.

3. With your hand, hold the paper clip and raise it up above the table until the string is taut.

4. Release the paper clip and observe its motion.

5. Stack the books on the table. Place the magnet so that one end extends over the edge of the top book. Position the books and magnet so that the magnet is over the paper clip.

6. Touch the end of the paper clip under the end of the magnet, then slowly pull the end of the string until the paper clip is suspended in the air and only slightly separated from the magnet.

7. With the paper clip suspended and separated from the magnet, cut the string and observe the motion of the paper clip.

Results   Without the magnet, the raised paper clip falls down toward the table when it is released. When the paper clip is suspended but separated from the magnet and the string is cut, the paper clip moves up toward the magnet.

Why? When the paper clip is raised with your hand, it has gravitational potential energy because of its position in Earth's gravitational force field. If the table is the reference point, then the gravitational potential energy depends on how high above the table the paper clip is raised. When an object with gravitational potential energy is free to move, the force of gravity acting upon it causes it to move toward the center of Earth. So when you released the paper clip, it moved in a direction that reduced its potential energy. This direction was down toward the table. The paper clip's gravitational potential energy (stored energy) was transformed into kinetic energy (energy of motion). Note that the paper clip moves in the direction of the force acting on it.

When the paper clip is held in a raised position above the table by the magnetic force of the magnet, it has two kinds of potential energy. One is gravitational potential energy due to being raised above the table. The other is magnetic potential energy due to the paper clip's position in the magnetic force field around the magnet. Since the magnetic force is toward the magnet, the two forces acting on the paper clip are in opposite directions. When the string was cut, the paper clip moved upward toward the magnet, which was the direction of the greater force. This motion caused the paper clip's magnetic potential energy to be decreased and its gravitational potential energy to be increased. The paper clip's magnetic potential energy was transformed into kinetic energy.

Solutions to Exercises

1. *Think!*

- Electrons in all atoms spin about their axis.
- Some electrons spin counterclockwise and others spin clockwise.
- A typical electron is paired with an electron with an opposite spin.
- Magnetic materials have unpaired electrons.
- Which figure shows an unpaired electron?

Figure A represents an unpaired electron found in magnetic material.

2. *Think!*

- Iron is a magnetic material.
- Magnetic materials contain domains.
- When magnetized, the domains of magnetic materials line up.
- Which figure represents lined-up domains?

Figure A represents magnetized iron.

20
Changers
Chemical Energy

What You Need to Know

Potential energy is due to the attraction or repulsion that objects or their parts have for each other. Atoms are made of charged particles (negatively charged electrons and positively charged nuclei) that attract and repel each other. Since opposite charges attract, negatively charged electrons and the positively charged nuclei within atoms attract each other. However, since like charges repel each other, electrons repel other electrons and atomic nuclei repel other atomic nuclei.

Chemical bonds are the attractive forces between atoms that enable the group to act as a unit. In the figure, straight lines

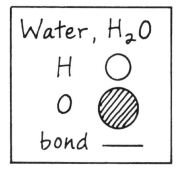

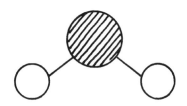

represent the bonds between atoms in the molecule for water. There is no actual physical attachment between the atoms, only an attractive force due to differences in the charged particles in the atoms.

The potential energy that substances have due to their bonds is called chemical potential energy or simply chemical energy. During a chemical reaction, one or more chemicals called reactants are changed into one or more new substances called products. The changes during a chemical reaction are due to the breaking and making of chemical bonds, which causes changes in chemical potential energy.

In **exothermic reactions**, the potential energy of the reactants is less than that of the products. The difference in energy is not destroyed; instead, it is transformed from chemical bond energy in the reactants to heat energy as a product. The products of an exothermic reaction are hotter than the reactants. If the reaction occurs in a container, the temperature of the mixture would rise due to this released heat. An equation that represents an exothermic reaction is:

$$A + B \rightarrow C + D + energy$$

The letters on the left side of the arrow, A and B, represent reactants, and the letters on the right side of the arrow, C and D, represent products. Energy is also a product. The burning of gasoline in a car is an example of an exothermic reaction. The heat energy produced is used to move the car.

In **endothermic reactions**, the potential energy of the products is greater than that of the reactants. Energy is not created; instead, energy, such as heat energy, is taken in and transformed into chemical bond energy. The products of an endothermic reaction are cooler than the reactants. If the reaction occurs in a container, the temperature of the mixture would decrease due to the heat being removed and used to form bonds. Thus, in an endothermic reaction, energy is a reactant. An equation that represents an endothermic reaction is:

$$A + B + energy \rightarrow C + D$$

An example of an endothermic reaction is the chemical reaction in green plants called **photosynthesis**, in which, in the presence of light, plants change carbon dioxide and water to **glucose** (sugar) and oxygen. The light energy is absorbed by special molecules in the plant called **chlorophyll**. The products, glucose and oxygen, have more potential energy than the reactants, carbon dioxide and water.

The law of conservation of energy holds true for chemical reactions. This law states that energy under normal conditions cannot be created or destroyed. Instead, it is just transformed from one kind to another. If heat energy is produced as a product in a chemical reaction, it is not created; it comes from stored energy within the reactants. Likewise, if the chemical energy of the product is less than the reactants, it is not destroyed but transformed into another kind of energy. The law of conservation of mass also holds true for chemical reactions. This law states that the total mass of the reactants in a chemical reaction equals the total mass of the products: bonds between atoms that make up the reactants are broken, and products with bonds between different combinations of the same atoms are formed.

Chemical energy is often converted to heat energy. But chemical energy is also converted to other forms of energy. For example, when something **burns**, which is the combination of a substance with oxygen, heat as well as light energy are generally released. Electricity is also the result of some chemical reactions. For example, the chemical reactions in a battery create electric energy.

Exercises

1. Which figure, A or B, represents an endothermic reaction?

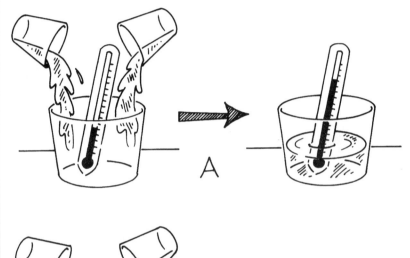

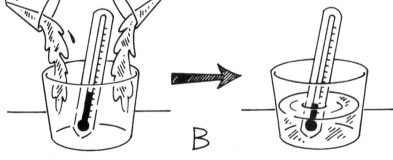

2. Which equation, A or B, represents the chemical reaction called photosynthesis?

   A. carbon dioxide + water + energy (light)
   → glucose + oxygen

   B. carbon dioxide + water
   → glucose + oxygen + energy (light)

3. Which figure, A or B, represents the law of conservation of mass?

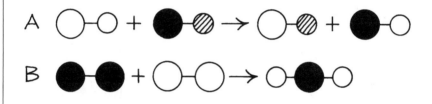

Activity: COOLER

Purpose To demonstrate an endothermic reaction.

Materials ½ cup (125 ml) vinegar
1-quart (1 L) jar
thermometer
2 tablespoons (30 ml) baking soda

Procedure

1. Pour the vinegar into the jar.

2. Stand the thermometer in the jar.

3. After 2 or more minutes, note the reading on the thermometer.

4. With the thermometer in the jar, add the baking soda.

5. Observe the thermometer and note whether the reading on the thermometer increased or decreased.

Results The temperature of the mixture decreases.

Why? Before adding the vinegar and baking soda together, they are about room temperature. When the vinegar and baking soda are mixed together, a chemical reaction occurs, resulting in products that include a gas. The foaming action indicates gas production. The temperature of the mixture decreases, which indicates that heat energy is taken out of the mixture. Thus, the reaction is an endothermic reaction in which energy is taken in and stored as potential energy in chemical bonds.

Solutions to Exercises

1. *Think!*

- Endothermic reactions take in energy and transform it into potential energy.

- The products of an endothermic reaction are cooler than the reactants.

- Which figure shows a decrease in temperature?

Figure B represents an endothermic reaction.

2. *Think!*

- Photosynthesis is an endothermic reaction that occurs in plants.

- Equations for endothermic reactions show energy combining with the reactants, which are on the left side of the arrow.

- The energy absorbed during photosynthesis comes from light energy.

- Which equation shows solar energy combined with the reactants?

Equation A represents photosynthesis.

3. *Think!*

- The law of conservation of mass states that a chemical reaction does not create or destroy mass.

- The mass is conserved in a chemical reaction because the number and kind of atoms that make up the reactants are the same for the products.

- Which figure represents the same number and kind of atoms for the reactants and products?

Figure A represents the law of conservation of mass.

21

Equal

Nuclear Energy

What You Need to Know

A nuclear reaction (changes in the nucleus of an atom) is similar to a chemical reaction in that reactants change, forming new products. The reactions are also alike in that the number of nucleons (nuclear particles, whether neutrons or protons) is conserved, which means the number of nucleons in the reactants is equal to the number of nucleons in the products. But the reactions differ in that **transmutation** (the change of one atom into another as a result of changes in the nucleus) occurs in nuclear reactions.

Three common nuclear reactions in which transmutation occurs are radioactive decay, fission, and fusion. During **radioactive decay**, a nucleus that is unstable (likely to change) **spontaneously** (happening by itself) emits high-energy radiation called **nuclear rays**, forming a new element. If this new element is unstable, it also decays. This spontaneous breakdown continues until a **stable** (not likely to change) nucleus is formed. The nuclei of **radioactive elements** undergo radioactive decay. The time it takes for half of the mass of a radioactive element to undergo radioactive decay is called its **half-life**. After one half-life, half of the atoms in the sample are those of the reactant (the original radioactive element) and the other half are those of the decay product (the new element). Two half-lives of a radioactive element are shown in the figure. During **nuclear fission**, a large nucleus is bombarded by a neutron, causing the nucleus to eject three neutrons when it splits into two roughly equal parts. During **nuclear fusion**, small nuclei combine to form a large nucleus.

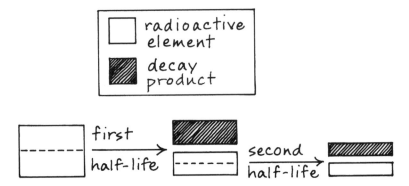

Another difference between chemical and nuclear reactions is that the mass of the nucleons is not conserved. The law of conservation of mass and energy states that the combined amount of mass and energy in the universe does not change. So the total mass and energy are the same, and any decrease in mass causes an increase in energy and vice versa. In nuclear reactions there are changes in the mass of nucleons, and this mass is changed into **nuclear energy** (energy released during a nuclear reaction). The German-born American physicist Albert Einstein (1879–1955) determined how to calculate the amount of energy produced when mass changes into energy. The equation he used is now called the **Einstein equation**, which is:

$$E = \Delta m c^2$$

In the Einstein equation, E is the nuclear energy produced; the delta sign (Δ) indicates a change in the factor following it, so Δm means a change in mass; and c is the speed of light. The speed of light is 186,000 miles (300,000 km) per second. The heat from fission reactions is used in a **nuclear reactor** (device to convert nuclear energy into useful forms of energy) to heat water to make steam, which is used to produce electricity.

Exercises

1. Radioactive elements are used to date rocks and fossils. Use the C-14 data table to determine the age of a fossil that contains 10 grams of carbon-14 (C-14) and 10 grams of nitrogen-14 (N-14).

Radioactive Element	Decay Product	Estimated Half-Life
carbon-14 (C-14)	nitrogen-14 (N-14)	5,730 years

2. Use the bar graph showing the radioactive decay of 100 grams of uranium-238 (U-238) to answer these questions:

a. What is the half-life of U-238?

b. If a rock contained 100 grams of U-238, how many grams of U-238 would be left in the rock after 9 billion years?

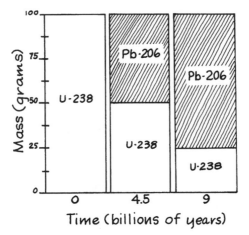

RADIOACTIVE DECAY OF U-238

Activity: HALF-TIME

Purpose   To model radioactive decay.

Materials   large bowl
scissors
sheet of copy paper

Procedure

1. Set the bowl on a table.

2. Count out 5 seconds by counting one thousand one, one thousand two, and so on, as you cut the paper in half. You need to estimate the line across the paper that divides it in half.

3. Place one of the paper halves in the bowl. Keep the other paper half and repeat step 2.

4. Continue to repeat steps 2 and 3 six times, or until the paper is too small to safely cut it.

5. To determine the number of half-lives represented, count the number of paper pieces in the bowl.

Results The paper is divided seven or more times.

Why? The time it takes for half of a radioactive element to change to another stable element is called its half-life. The half-life in this activity is 5 seconds. At the end of 5 seconds, half of the paper was placed in the bowl to demonstrate the change that half of the radioactive material had decayed to a stable material. After another 5 seconds, half of the remaining sheet was placed in the bowl. As time passed, the amount of material in the bowl increased and the amount out of the bowl decreased, just as all radioactive elements will eventually decrease. While the half-life in this activity was 5 seconds, the half-lives of some radioactive elements are much shorter, whereas others are hours, days, years, or even billions of years.

Solutions to Exercises

1. *Think!*

- How does the mass of C-14 compare to N-14? Their masses are equal.

- Equal masses of a radioactive element and its decay product indicate that a period of time equal to one half-life has passed.

- What is the half-life of C-14?

The fossil would be about 5,730 years old.

2a. *Think!*

- Which period of time shows that half of the U-238 has decayed?

The half-life of U-238 is 4.5 billion years.

b. *Think!*

- Find the bar above 9 billion years and place your finger on the line above the U-238 section of the bar.

- Move your finger to the left until it touches the mass scale of the graph. What mass reading does your finger touch?

There would be 25 grams of U-238 left in the rock after 9 billion years.

22

Used Up

Nonrenewable Energy Resources

What You Need to Know

Resources are all the natural materials and features of Earth that help support life and satisfy people's needs. Materials that are available in nature to produce energy are called **natural energy resources**. If the resource can be reused, which means it is **recycled**, such as water and air, it is called a **renewable energy resource**. Resources that are used only once, which means they are not recycled, such as fossil fuels, are called **nonrenewable energy resources**.

The term **fuel** is generally limited to those substances that can burn. Coal, oil, and natural gas are known as **fossil fuels** (energy-rich material formed from long-buried prehistoric organisms). They have a high carbon content and readily burn. Much of the coal used today is burned to produce electricity. The basic process from coal to electricity is: (1) Coal, which has chemical potential energy, burns and produces thermal energy. (2) Thermal energy is used to heat water, producing steam. (3) The steam turns turbines (fanlike devices) in generators in electric power plants. (4) Generators change the kinetic mechanical energy of the turbines into electricity.

Fossil fuels can be thought of as forms of buried sunshine because the chemical potential energy stored in fossil fuels can be traced back to solar energy. Through photosynthesis, plants use solar energy to produce glucose, which is considered the basic energy source for all organisms. Plants use much of this glucose as an energy source, and the extra glucose is changed into other chemicals, such as starch for storage. Animals eat plants and change the stored chemicals back into glucose, which is used in an energy-producing process called respiration. Fossil fuels are the chemical remains of plants and animals that depended on photosynthesis millions of years ago. When burned, the chemical potential energy in fossil fuels is transformed into other forms of energy, including light and heat. So the energy released by burning fossil fuel was originally captured from sunlight during photosynthesis. Thus, basically all life on Earth, directly or indirectly, depends on photosynthesis as a source of energy, making it one of the most important chemical energy–producing processes known.

Fossil fuel energy, as well as chemical energy, are both examples of potential energy, which can be compared to the potential energy stored in a compressed spring. Coal is a fossil fuel in which chemical energy is stored in the bonds between carbon atoms. In the diagram, the chemical energy in coal is compared to the energy stored in the compressed spring. When the spring is sprung, the coils rapidly separate and the spring returns to a lower-energy, more stable (not likely to change) state. The energy that was stored in the compressed spring is released during this process, just like the energy in the coal is released when it is burned.

Likewise, solar energy is indirectly stored in the chemical compounds making up fossil fuels. During the burning of fossil fuels, the atoms rearrange to form more stable structures, and some of the stored energy is released in the form of heat and light.

Fossil fuels are not renewable. Their supply is limited for several reasons, including the fact that it took millions of years for them to form. It is believed that conditions for the formation of fossil fuels are no longer present, but since the process is so slow, no one can observe and identify the different stages of formation.

A

coiled spring   fossil fuel (coal)

B

sprung spring   burning fuel

Exercises

Use diagrams A, B, and C to answer the following questions:

1. Which diagram, A, B, or C, represents energy stored in fossil fuels?

2. Which diagram, A, B, or C, represents energy being released when a fossil fuel is burned?

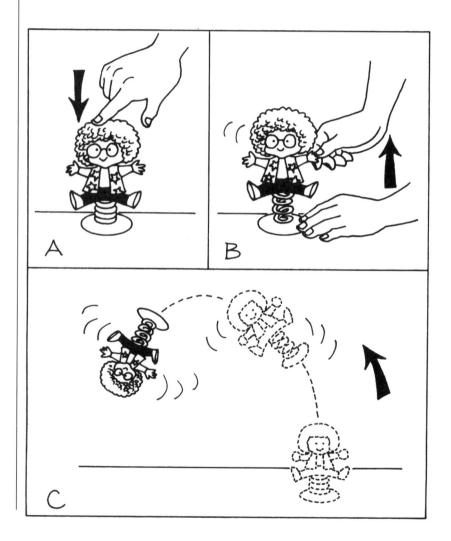

Activity: COLLECTORS

Purpose   To demonstrate how natural gas rises.

Materials   ¼ cup (63 ml) tap water
½-pint (250-ml) plastic bottle, such as a water bottle
¼ cup (63 ml) cooking oil
1 effervescent tablet, such as Alka-Seltzer
9-inch (22.5 cm) round balloon

Procedure

1. Pour the water into the bottle.

2. Pour the oil into the bottle.

3. Break the effervescent tablet in half and drop the two pieces into the bottle. Immediately stretch the mouth of the balloon over the opening in the bottle.

4. Observe the contents of the bottle and the balloon.

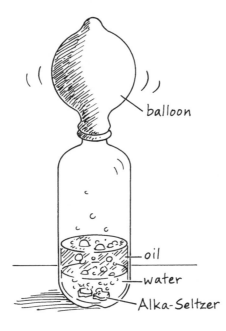

Results A gas produced in the water moved upward through the oil. The gas partially inflated the balloon.

Why? Oil and natural gas formed from prehistoric organisms that lived in the ocean millions of years ago. The parts of these organisms that collected on the ocean floor were slowly buried and compressed under layers of sediment. Heat and pressure changed the **sediment** (rock particle transported and deposited by water, wind, or glaciers) into rock and the remains of the organisms into oil and natural gas.

In areas with **porous** (having holes) rock, the oil and gas slowly filled the tiny holes in the rock. This porous rock was called **reservoir rock** by **geologists** (scientists who study Earth) because oil and natural gas collected and were stored in it. Because the holes in the reservoir rock were usually filled with water, the less dense oil and gas, which are not soluble in water, moved upward through the water in the rock. When the oil and gas reached a **nonporous** (without holes) rock, such as shale, the oil and gas collected below it. Natural gas is usually found in pools above oil because it is less dense than oil, as you can see from this experiment. Enough gas collected above the oil in this experiment to partially inflate the balloon.

Solutions to Exercises

1. *Think!*

- Fossil fuels contain stored energy in the form of chemical energy. This energy can be compared to a compressed spring because they both have potential energy (energy due to position or condition).

- Which diagram shows a compressed spring?

Diagram A represents energy stored in fossil fuels.

2. *Think!*

- When a fossil fuel is burned, some of the stored chemical energy is released in the form of heat and light.

- When the spring is sprung, the coils rapidly separate and the energy that was stored in the compressed spring is quickly released during this process. This is similar to the way energy is released when fossil fuels are burned.

- Which diagram, A, B, or C, shows a spring being sprung?

Diagram C represents energy released when a fossil fuel is burned.

23

Recycle

Renewable Energy Resources

What You Need to Know

Energy resources that can be recycled (reused), such as air and water or replaced, such as plants and animals, are called renewable. Plants and animals supply chemical energy (food) that is used by your body to grow and change. They are renewable because they can **reproduce** (produce new organisms like themselves).

Water can be used again and again because of the natural process called the **water cycle** (continuous interchange of water between the ocean, the land, plants, and the atmosphere). There are two basic changes in the water cycle. One is **evaporation**, which is the process by which a liquid changes to a gas as a result of being heated. The second change is **condensation**, which is the process by which a gas changes to a liquid as a result of being cooled. In the water cycle, water evaporates from Earth, condenses in the atmosphere, and falls as **precipitation** (the falling of water from the atmosphere in the form of rain, hail, snow, or sleet). One way that water is used as an energy source is in making **hydroelectric energy**, which is electric energy produced by falling water and a **generator** (a machine that changes natural energy, such as running water or wind, into electricity).

Air in motion, which is commonly called **wind**, provides the energy to turn machines such as a **windmill** (machine that converts wind into useful energy). The gases in air, including carbon dioxide and oxygen, provide chemical energy. Carbon dioxide is used by plants in the process called photosynthesis to produce food in the form of a sugar molecule called glucose and oxygen. Oxygen is used by animals and plants in the process called **respiration** to change food into energy and release carbon dioxide into the atmosphere. Plants and animals depend on glucose as an energy source. But animals are unable to produce glucose and must get it by eating plants. Also, the oxygen you breathe is released during photosynthesis. So you and animals depend on plants for glucose and oxygen. The exchange of oxygen and carbon dioxide between plants and animals is called the **oxygen–carbon dioxide cycle**. Like the water cycle, the atoms involved in this cycle are continuously being separated and recombined, so they are used over and over again.

Oxygen – Carbon Dioxide Cycle

Exercises

1. Study the diagrams on page 173 to answer the following:

   a. How many of the diagrams, A, B, C, and D, represent respiration?

b. How many of the diagrams, A, B, C, and D, represent photosynthesis?

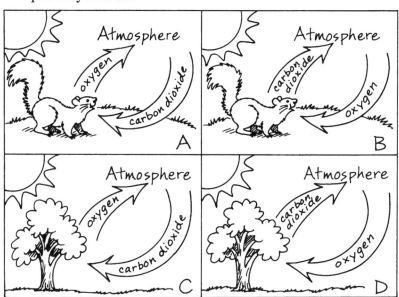

2. In the diagram, which of the four arrows, 1, 2, 3, and 4, represent the carbon dioxide–oxygen cycle?

Activity: All Alone

Purpose   To demonstrate that plants can recycle material needed for food and energy.

Materials   ½ cup (125 ml) small gravel
1-quart (1-L) large-mouthed plastic jar with lid
1 cup (250 ml) potting soil
iced-tea spoon
small plant that will fit inside the jar, such as very small fern, miniature African violet, wandering Jew, ivy
½ cup (125 ml) tap water
paper towel

Procedure

1. Pour the gravel into the jar. Shake the jar gently to evenly spread the gravel.

2. Pour the soil into the jar and again shake to evenly spread the soil.

3. Use the spoon to dig a hole in the soil equal to the size of the plant's roots.

4. Set the plant in the hole in the soil. With the spoon, cover the plant's roots with soil and press the soil firmly around the plant. Take care not to damage the plant's roots.

5. Pour the water on the plant.

6. Use the paper towel to clean the inside surface of the jar above the soil.

7. Seal the jar with the lid.

8. Set the jar in a lighted area but out of direct sunlight.

9. Observe the contents of the jar periodically for 2 days.

If the inside of the jar is continuously covered with water, open the jar, dry the water with a paper towel, and close the jar again.

10. Observe the contents of the jar periodically for 4 or more weeks.

Results The inside of the jar appears cloudy at times and the plant grows.

Why? Potted plants can live in a closed container for a time as long as they have access to light. This is because plants are **autotrophs** (organisms that can make their own food). Plants recycle materials needed for food and energy production. During photosynthesis in plants, carbon dioxide and water are changed to glucose, oxygen, and water. During respiration, the glucose, oxygen, and water are changed back to carbon dioxide and water plus energy. Plants do need access to light, however, because light energy cannot be recycled.

Solutions to Exercises

1a. *Think!*

- During respiration, plants and animals take in oxygen and give out carbon dioxide.
- Diagram B shows an animal taking in oxygen and giving out carbon dioxide.
- Diagram D shows a plant taking in oxygen and giving out carbon dioxide.

Two diagrams, B and D, represent respiration.

b. *Think!*

- During photosynthesis, plants take in carbon dioxide and give out oxygen.
- Diagram C shows a plant taking in carbon dioxide and giving out oxygen.

One diagram, C, represents photosynthesis.

2. *Think!*

- During the carbon dioxide–oxygen cycle, animals take in oxygen that is given out by plants, and plants take in carbon dioxide that is given out by animals.
- Which arrow shows oxygen being lost by the tree and taken in by the girl?
- Which arrow shows carbon dioxide being lost by the girl and taken in by the tree?

Arrows 2 and 4 correctly represent the carbon dioxide–oxygen cycle.

24

Collectors

Direct Heating by Solar Energy

What You Need to Know

Solar energy is radiant energy from the Sun. This energy travels through space to Earth in the form of electromagnetic waves. In an hour, the Sun sends as much or more energy as people use to run factories, machines, and vehicles and to heat buildings for a year. But only a small part of this direct solar energy can be collected and used because the solar energy is so spread out over the surface of Earth. Most of the solar energy that reaches Earth's surface is in the form of visible light.

The two methods of directly using solar energy to heat buildings and homes are passive solar heating and active solar heating. **Passive solar heating** is a method of heating with solar energy that does not require mechanical power to circulate heat. Instead, structural designs are used that help to absorb solar energy and allow the heat to circulate by natural convection. For example, during the year as Earth **revolves** (moves in a curved path around another object) around the Sun, because Earth's axis is tilted in relation to the Sun, the apparent path of the Sun across the sky is lower in the winter and higher in the summer. So buildings in the Northern Hemisphere with large windows facing south allow more sunlight to enter a room than windows facing other directions. To prevent overheating in the summer, overhangs on buildings block some of the summer (high-angle) sunlight. They also allow more of the winter (low-angle) sunlight to enter and warm rooms. Another technique is to build a wall of special energy-absorbing material that is painted black on the inside of the house. Black materials absorb more solar energy than other colors. This wall absorbs solar energy, heats up, then radiates this heat, warming the house during the day and into the night.

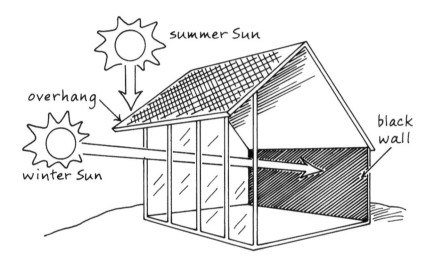

Another example of a passive solar energy system is a **solar oven**, which is a device that uses sunlight to cook food. The simplest oven might be a metal box that gets hot inside because sunlight heats the metal, or it might be a closed jar containing a liquid that heats because of sunlight hitting the jar. Some solar ovens use mirrors and/or lenses to focus sunlight onto the food.

Active solar heating is a method of heating with solar energy that requires mechanical power, such as pumps and fans, to circulate heat from solar collectors. A common solar collector is the flat-plate collector. It has a black metal plate in a box with a glass cover. Tubes filled with a liquid lie on the metal plate and are connected to pipes that carry the liquid through a building. The black metal plate absorbs heat from sunlight and heats the liquid in the tubes. A pump moves the heated liquid through a pipe, which runs through a container of water called a heat exchanger. Here the heat from the hot fluid in the pipe is transferred to the water. The cooler water in the pipe is then pumped back to the collector, where it is reheated. The hot water in the heat exchanger is transferred to a storage tank for later use and cooler water is pumped into the exchanger to be heated. The hot water in the storage tank is pumped through pipes to different parts of the house, including faucets and heaters. In a heater, some of the thermal energy of the water is lost as infrared radiation, and some is lost as heat is transferred by conduction to the air surrounding the heater. The heated air transfers heat throughout the room by convection.

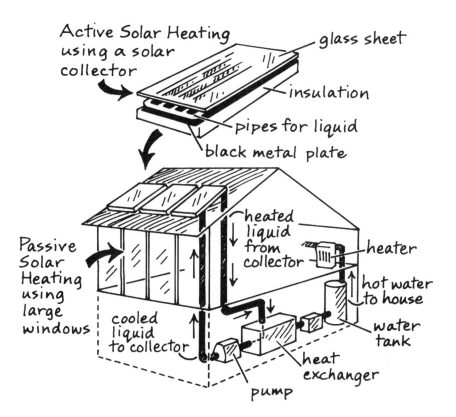

Exercises

1. Unscramble these words that relate to solar energy:
lrsoa nvoe
sipasev lorsa tganeih
viaect orlsa ghateni

2. In the figure, the container of water acts like a lens to focus sunlight onto the food. Which of the unscrambled words from Exercise 1 does the figure represent?

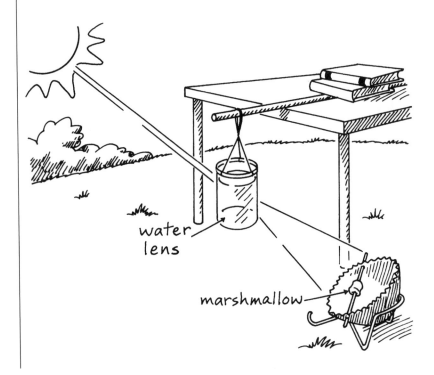

water lens

marshmallow

Activity: SUN TEA

Purpose To use passive solar heating for cooking.

Materials 1-quart (1-L) plastic jar with lid
dishwashing soap

tap water
2 tea bags
sugar or other sweetener (optional)

Procedure

1. Clean the jar with soap and water. Rinse the jar well with water.

2. Place the tea bags in the jar.

3. Fill the jar three-fourths full with water.

4. Place the lid on the jar and set it outdoors in an area where the jar will receive direct sunlight.

5. Observe the contents of the jar every 30 minutes for 2 hours.

6. If the jar was properly cleaned and clean tea bags and water were used, then, if you wish, you may drink the tea. Add sugar or sweetener as desired.

Results The tea bags float in the water. After 30 minutes the water around the tea bags was colored a pale brown, but the water below was uncolored. As time passed, more of the water became colored below the tea bags until all of the water was colored. The color of the water became darker with time.

Why? Solar energy strikes the jar and warms it. Heat from the molecules in the jar is transferred to the water by conduction. The solar energy also passes through the glass and directly warms the water inside, and heat is transferred from one water molecule to others by conduction. Chemicals in the tea dissolve in the warm water at the top of the jar that is in contact with the tea bags. The concentrated tea solution (a mixture of something in a liquid) at the top of the jar **disperses** (moves evenly throughout) in the water below. Any difference in the temperature of the water in the jar will also create convection currents (the rising of warm fluids and sinking of cooler fluids) that will further mix the tea solution.

Solutions to Exercises

1. *Think!*

lrsoa nvoe	SOLAR OVEN
sipasev lorsa tganeih	PASSIVE SOLAR HEATING
viaect orlsa ghateni	ACTIVE SOLAR HEATING

2. *Think!*

- What device is used to focus sunlight in order to heat materials such as food? A solar oven.

- The food is heated by direct sunlight that is transferred throughout the food by conduction, which means that one molecule bumps into the other, thus transferring energy. What method uses solar energy to heat a material using conduction to transfer the heat? Passive solar heating.

The figure represents a solar oven, which uses passive solar energy to heat materials such as the marshmallow.

25

Pass It On

Energy Transfers within a Community

What You Need to Know

Ecology is the study of how organisms relate to each other, as well as to nonliving things within their **environment** (all the living or nonliving surroundings of an organism). An **ecosystem** is the interaction of living and nonliving things in a given area. The levels of living things within an ecosystem start with individual organisms. The grouping of organisms of the same **species** (a group of organisms that are alike, such as roses or dogs) is called a **population**. All the populations within an ecosystem are called a **community**.

Energy enters an ecosystem through the process of photosynthesis carried on by plants. Through photosynthesis, energy is transformed from light energy into the chemical energy of food molecules in plants. Since plants can use energy from the Sun and nutrients from the soil and air to make their own food, they are called the **producers** of an ecosystem. Organisms in an ecosystem that cannot make their own food and must obtain their food by eating it are called **heterotrophs**. These organisms are called **consumers** (organisms that feed on other organisms).

Producers provide food for **primary consumers**, which are generally **herbivores** (animals that eat only plants). Primary consumers are eaten by **secondary consumers**; thus, these consumers are **carnivores** (animals that eat other animals).

Secondary consumers are eaten by **tertiary consumers**, which are eaten by **quarternary consumers**, and so on, with each level of consumer numbered in order. The final carnivore is called the **ultimate** or **top consumer**. The top consumers, as well as those that escape being eaten, eventually die and are consumed by **decomposers** (organisms that cause dead organisms to **decompose**—to rot or decay). Decomposers include some bacteria and fungi. The remains of the decomposed material provide nutrients for plants and are thus recycled. Each step along the feeding pathway is called a **trophic level** (each step in a food chain), with the producers being step 1 and the decomposers being the last step. Energy and nutrients flow as food passes from one trophic level to the next. The trophic level numbers indicate the order of the energy flow.

Consumers generally eat other consumers at a lower trophic level. An **omnivore** is a consumer that will eat both plants and animals, so it belongs to more than one trophic level. It is a primary consumer and can be a higher-level consumer, depending on the trophic level of animals it eats.

The single path of the transfer of energy from one organism to another within an ecosystem is called a **food chain**. The food chain diagram shown here gives one example of how organisms are linked together in the order in which they feed on each other. The links of this food chain are sunlight, periwinkle plants, a butterfly, a frog, a snake, a hawk, and bacteria and fungi. The food chain begins with sunlight, which is the starting source of energy in most ecosystems. Sunlight provides the energy necessary for the plant to produce food by photosynthesis. Parts of the plant are eaten by the butterfly, the butterfly is eaten by the frog, and the frog is eaten by the snake, which is eaten by the hawk. The hawk is the top carnivore. The decomposers eat the plants and animals that die.

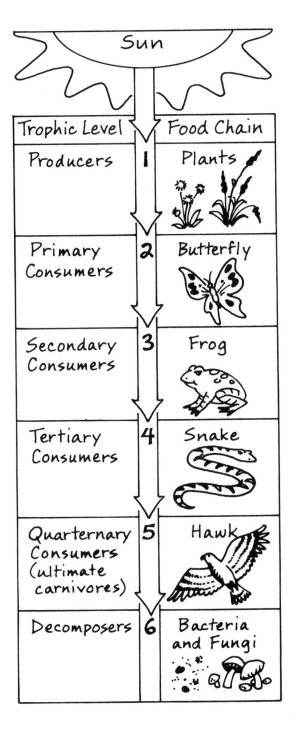

A food chain represents one possible pathway for energy to be transferred in an ecosystem. However, there are many different routes. Generally a species, such as the frog, doesn't eat only one thing. The frog might eat a grasshopper instead of a butterfly, or the hawk might eat a mouse instead of a snake. The interconnections of food chains within an ecosystem make up a **food web**.

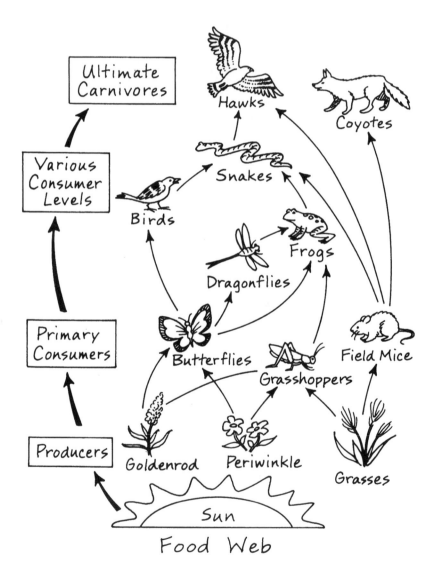

Food Web

Exercises

The amount of energy available for use by each link of a food chain varies. Use the Food Chain bar graph to answer the following:

1. Which kind of organism, plant or animal, has the most available energy for use?

2. Does an herbivore have more or less available energy than a carnivore?

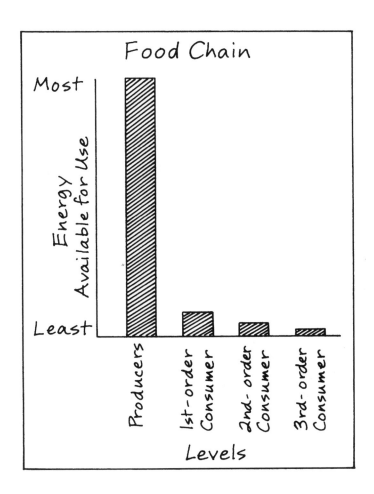

3. Which diagram, A or B, represents a food chain?

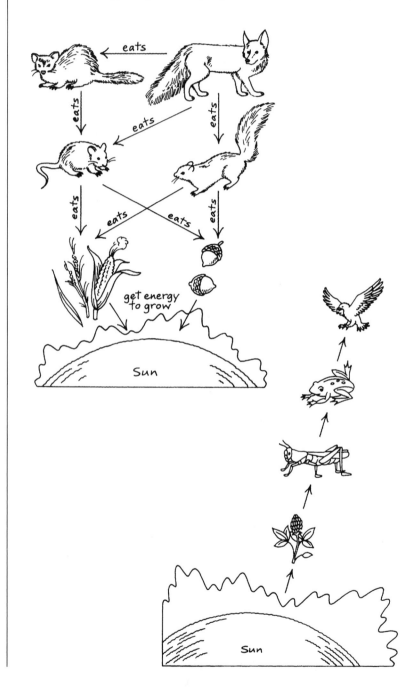

Activity: TOP TO BOTTOM

Purpose To model an energy pyramid in an ecosystem.

Materials sheet of copy paper
scissors
pen
ruler
transparent tape

Procedure

1. Fold the paper as shown with its top edge against an adjacent side. Crease the fold by pressing it flat with your fingers. Cut off the bottom strip from the paper and discard.

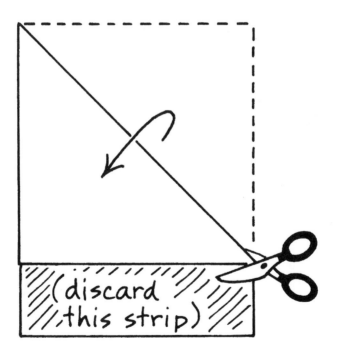

2. Unfold the paper and refold it diagonally the opposite way. Crease the fold as before.

3. Open the paper. Using the pen and the ruler, divide three of the four triangles made by the fold lines into four sections as shown.

4. In section A, write the levels of a food chain as shown: producer, 1st-order consumer, 2nd-order consumer, 3rd-order consumer. In sections B and C, give examples of the different levels of a food chain. Two food-chain examples are shown. You may wish to add drawings or pictures cut from magazines.

5. Cut along the fold line separating sections A and D to the center of the paper as shown.

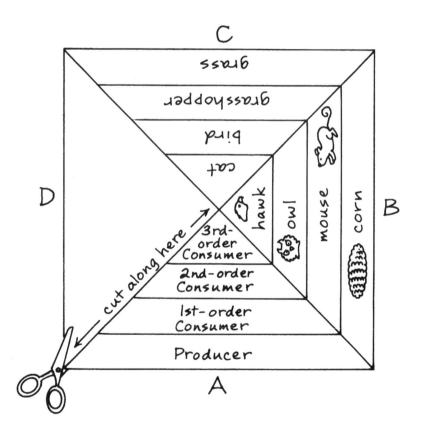

6. Overlap section D with section A. Secure them together with tape. Stand the paper structure on its open base and you have a pyramid.

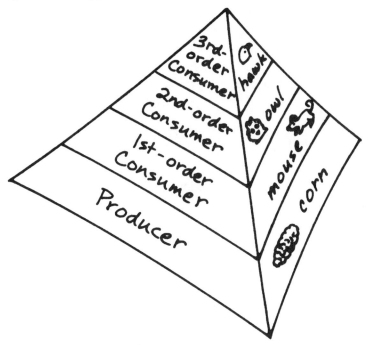

Results You have made a model of the pyramid of energy in an ecosystem.

Why? Plants produce food, which is chemical potential energy. Only about 10 percent of the food energy produced by plants is available to first-order consumers (herbivores). Of the remaining 90 percent of the energy, about half is used for life functions and the rest is lost as heat during respiration. Similarly, only about 10 percent of the food energy that makes up the body of an herbivore is available to the next level, the carnivore, and about 10 percent of the food energy of the carnivore is passed on to the omnivore. The exact percentage from one level to the next will vary with the organisms. The general pattern showing the amount of food passed from producers to herbivores to carnivores and/or omnivores forms an **energy pyramid**, with the first level being the producers. Each level of an energy pyramid, as shown in this activity, from the producer to the top consumer (the top consumer in a food chain), has less available energy represented by the decreasing size of the layers.

Solutions to Exercises

1. *Think!*

   - Which level has the tallest bar on the graph? Producers.

   - What kind of organism is a producer? Plants are called producers because they produce their own energy.

   Plants have the most energy available to them.

2. *Think!*

   - What are the food-chain levels for an herbivore and a carnivore? An herbivore eats only plants and is a first-order consumer; a carnivore eats only meat and is a second-order or higher-order consumer.

   - Which has a higher bar on the graph, a first-order consumer or a second-order or higher-order consumer?

   First-order consumers have more available energy for use than second-order or higher-order consumers.

3. *Think!*

   - A food chain is a single pathway of how energy is transferred through an ecosystem by the eating of one organism by another. A food web is the interconnection of different food chains within an ecosystem.

- Which diagram shows one single pathway of how organisms are linked together in the order in which they feed on each other?

Diagram B represents a food chain.

Glossary

absorb To take in.

active solar heating A method of heating with solar energy that requires mechanical power, such as pumps and fans to circulate heat from solar collectors.

air The mixture of gases making up Earth's atmosphere.

alloy A material, such as steel, made of the blending of two or more elements, at least one being a metal.

ampere (A) A unit for measuring current; called amp for short. One amp (1 A) equals 6.25×10^{18} electric charges per second.

amplitude In reference to a wave, the maximum movement of the particles of a medium from their resting position.

antinodes The crests and troughs of a standing wave.

atmosphere In reference to Earth, the blanket of air surrounding Earth.

atom The building block of matter; the smallest part of an element that has all the properties of that element.

attraction Pulling together.

autotrophs Organisms that can make their own food.

battery A device that changes chemical energy into electrical potential energy; technically made of two or more electric cells but also the common name for some single electric cells, such as flashlight batteries.

bond The force holding atoms together.

burn The chemical reaction that involves the fast combination of a substance with oxygen. Heat as well as light energy are generally produced.

carnivores Meat eaters.

Celsius scale A thermometer scale named after the Swedish scientist Anders Celsius (1701–1744). The unit of temperature on the Celsius scale is the degree Celsius, °C.

charge The property of particles within atoms that causes a force between the particles; also called **electric charge**.

charging by conduction The method of electrically charging a neutral object by touching it with a charged object.

charging by friction The process of charging two neutrally charged materials by rubbing the materials together.

chemical energy A form of potential energy; energy in the bonds that hold atoms together; also called chemical potential energy.

chemical potential energy Chemical energy.

chemical reaction The process in which substances change into new substances.

chlorophyll Special molecules in plants that absorb light energy necessary for photosynthesis.

community All the populations within an ecosystem.

compound Two or more different kinds of atoms linked together by bonds. See also **ionic compound** and **molecular compound**.

compression The region in longitudinal waves where the particles of the medium are squeezed closer together.

concentration The measure of the amount of substance in an area.

condensation The process by which a gas changes to a liquid as a result of being cooled.

conduction The process of transferring heat or electrical energy from one particle to another by collisions of the particles. See also **electrical conduction** and **thermal conduction**.

conductors Substances that easily transfer heat or electricity; materials with a high concentration of free electrons. See also **electrical conductor** and **thermal conductor**.

conserved Remains constant.

constellation A group of stars that appear to form a pattern.

consumers Organisms that feed on other organisms; heterotrophs.

convection The method in which heat is transferred by means of movement of heated fluids.

convection current The up-and-down movement of fluids due to differences in density as a result of differences in temperature.

crest The high part of a transverse wave.

current The measure of the amount of electric charge per second moving through a conductor; measured in amperes.

current electricity Electricity due to the movement of electric charges; electrical energy due to the movement of free electrons; also called a **current**.

decibel (db) The unit of measuring sound intensity.

decompose To rot or decay; the breakup of chemicals in dead organisms into smaller parts.

decomposers Organisms that cause dead organisms to decompose.

dense Parts are close together.

density The number of particles in an area; measure of the mass per volume of a substance; measure of the compactness of a substance.

diffuse To spread in all directions.

disperse To spread evenly throughout.

displacement Taken out of the normal position.

dry cell An electric cell with a chemical paste as an electrolyte, such as in a flashlight battery.

ecology The study of how organisms relate to each other as well as to nonliving things within their environment.

ecosystem The interaction of living and nonliving things in a given area.

Einstein equation $E = \Delta mc^2$.

elastic potential energy Energy of materials in a state of being stretched or twisted.

electric cell A device that changes chemical energy into electrical energy.

electric charge See **charge**.

electric circuit The path through which electric charges move.

electric conduction The process of transferring electrical energy associated with current electricity through a conductor due to the movement of free electrons in the material.

electric conductor Material through which electric charges easily move; material that easily conducts electrical current.

electric energy Energy associated with electricity. See **potential electric energy**.

electric field The region around a charged particle in which a force acts on an electric charge brought into the region.

electric insulator Name of an insulator when referring to its ability to restrict the conduction of electric charges.

electricity   A form of energy due to static or moving charges. See also **current electricity** and **static electricity**.

electrode   In reference to an electric cell, a conductor in the cell that collects or gives up electrons.

electrolyte   A mixture of chemicals that produces a chemical reaction in which electric charges are released.

electromagnetic spectrum   The different types of radiation arranged in order of energy including ultraviolet radiation and visible light.

electromagnetic waves   Waves that do not require a medium and can travel through space, such as light, microwaves, and X rays.

electron   A negatively charged particle found outside the nucleus of an atom.

electrostatic induction   The process of polarizing a neutral material by separating its positive and negative charges due to the proximity (nearness) of a charged object.

electrostatics   The study of the cause, nature, behavior, and uses of static electricity.

element   The basic chemical substance of which all things are made; composed of only one kind of atom.

endothermic reaction   A chemical reaction in which the chemical energy of the products is more than that of the reactants; a chemical reaction in which heat is a reactant.

energy   The ability to do work.

energy levels   A model used to compare the energy of electrons in an atom. They are the regions around and at different distances from the nucleus of an atom.

energy pyramid   The general pattern showing the amount of food passed from producers to herbivores to carnivores and/or omnivores.

environment   All the living and nonliving surroundings of an organism.

evaporation   The process by which a liquid changes to a gas as a result of being heated.

excited state   The energy level of an electron in an atom that is greater than its normal energy level, which is ground state.

exothermic reaction   A chemical reaction in which the chemical energy of the bonds in the products is less than the chemical energy in the reactants; a chemical reaction in which heat is a product.

Fahrenheit scale   A thermometer scale named after the German scientist Daniel Gabriel Fahrenheit (1686–1736). The unit of temperature on the Fahrenheit scale is the degree Fahrenheit, °F.

filament   A small-diameter wire in incandescent lamps; it is generally made of the metal tungsten.

fluid   Any liquid or gaseous material that can move freely.

food chain   The single path of the transfer of energy from one organism within an ecosystem.

food web   The interconnections of food chains within an ecosystem.

foot   An English unit of distance.

foot-pound (ft-lb)   An English unit of work.

force (f)   A push or pull on an object.

force field   A region that exerts a force of attraction or repulsion on an object in it.

fossil fuels   Energy-rich materials formed from long-buried prehistoric organisms that can burn, such as coal, oil, and natural gas.

free electrons   Electrons in some solids, particularly metals, that are not tightly bound to a single atom and are relatively free to move through the solid.

frequency In reference to waves, the number of waves per unit of time.

friction The force that opposes the motion of two surfaces in contact with each other; a method of producing static electricity.

fuel A term generally limited to those substances that can burn.

gamma rays Invisible radiation produced in nuclear reactions.

generator A machine that changes natural energy, such as running water or wind, into electricity.

geologists Scientists who study Earth.

glucose A type of sugar produced during photosynthesis.

gram (g) A metric unit for measuring mass.

gravitational force field In reference to Earth, it is a region that attracts objects toward Earth.

gravitational potential energy Potential energy that depends on the position of an object within Earth's gravitational field.

gravity The force that exists between objects due to their mass.

ground state The normal energy level of a specific electron in an atom.

half-life The time it takes for half of the mass of a radioactive element to undergo radioactive decay.

heat The energy that flows from a warm material to a cool material due to differences in temperature; energy transferred by conduction, convection, or radiation.

herbivores Plant eaters.

hertz (Hz) A metric unit for frequency.

heterotrophs Organisms that cannot make their own food.

humidity   The amount of water vapor in air.

hydroelectric energy   Electric energy produced by falling water and a generator.

incandescent lamp   A lamp whose light bulb produces light by heating a filament to a high temperature.

infrared radiation   Invisible radiation that is felt as heat, and its wave size is greater than red light; heat waves.

inertia   The tendency of an object in motion to continue to move forward.

insulator   A substance that is a poor conductor; a material with a low concentration of free electrons. See also **electric insulator** and **thermal insulator**.

intensity   In reference to a wave, the amount of wave energy per second.

ion   An atom or a group of atoms with an electric charge.

ionic compound   A compound made up of ions.

joule (J)   A newton-meter work unit in the metric system.

kinetic energy (KE)   Energy that a moving object has because of its motion.

law of conservation of energy   The law that states energy under normal circumstances cannot be created or destroyed; instead, it is transformed from one kind of energy to another.

law of conservation of mass   The law that states under ordinary chemical reactions matter cannot be created or destroyed; it only changes forms. The total amount of matter in a chemical reaction remains constant.

law of conservation of mass and energy   The law that states that the combined amount of mass and energy in the universe does not change.

law of conservation of mechanical energy   The law that states the sum of the mechanical potential energy and the mechanical kinetic energy of an object remains the same as long as no outside force, such as friction, acts on it.

law of electric charges   The law that states like charges repel each other and unlike charges attract each other.

law of magnetic poles   The law that states like poles of a magnet repel each other and unlike poles of a magnet attract each other.

lightning   The visible static discharge between clouds or a cloud and Earth.

lines of force   In reference to a diagram representing an electric field, the lines drawn to visualize the presence of the electric field around a charge.

longitudinal wave   A wave in which the displacement is parallel to the motion of the wave.

machine   A device that helps you do work.

magnet   An object made of magnetic material that produces a magnetic field.

magnetic domain   A group of atoms with unpaired electrons that has a single magnetic field around it; a group of atoms that acts like a microscopic magnet with a magnetic material.

magnetic field   A region around a magnet where its magnetic force affects other magnetic material.

magnetic force   The force of attraction or repulsion between two magnets, or the force of attraction between a magnet and a magnetic material; the force produced by the motion of electric charges.

magnetic material   A material attracted to a magnet as well as material that magnets are made of.

magnetic poles   The regions of a magnet where the magnetic forces appear strongest; names of poles are north pole and south pole.

magnetic potential energy The energy of an object that has the ability to do work because of its position in a magnetic field.

magnetism The term that describes all effects of a magnetic field, including magnetic potential energy.

magnetized To cause a material to have a magnetic field; occurs when most of the domains in a magnetic material line up in the same direction.

mass The amount of material in a substance; measured in grams.

matter The stuff that the universe is made of; anything that takes up space and has mass.

mechanical energy The energy of motion; the energy of an object that is moving or has the potential of moving.

mechanical kinetic energy A form of mechanical energy in which the energy of an object is due to the motion of the object.

mechanical potential energy (PE_{ma}) A form of mechanical energy in which the energy of an object is due to its position or condition.

mechanical waves Waves that require a medium, such as water waves and sound waves.

medium A substance through which mechanical waves can travel.

meter (m) A metric unit for measuring distance.

microwave A low-energy radiant energy used in cooking food and in communication.

mnemonic A memory device.

molecular compound A compound made up of molecules.

molecule The smallest physical unit of a compound.

natural energy resources Materials that are available in nature to produce energy.

negative terminal   A terminal with a negative charge.

neutral   In reference to atoms, having a balanced number of positive and negative charges.

neutron   A particle in the nucleus of an atom with no charge.

newton (N)   A metric unit for measuring force.

nodes   Points on a wave that are not displaced from the resting position.

nonmagnetic material   A material in which the electrons in the atoms are paired.

nonporous   Without holes.

nonrenewable energy resource   A natural resource that can be used only once, which means it is not recycled, such as fossil fuels.

nuclear energy   Energy released during a nuclear reaction.

nuclear fission   A nuclear reaction in which a large nucleus is bombarded by a neutron, causing the nucleus to eject three neutrons, and the nucleus splits into two roughly equal parts.

nuclear fusion   A nuclear reaction in which small nuclei combine to form a large nucleus.

nuclear potential energy   Energy stored in the nucleus of an atom.

nuclear rays   High-energy radiation emitted during a nuclear reaction.

nuclear reaction   A reaction involving changes in a nucleus; the nucleus of a reactant changes, forming a new element.

nuclear reactor   A device to convert nuclear energy into useful forms of energy.

nucleons   Nuclear particles, such as protons and neutrons.

nucleus   The center part of an atom.

omnivores   Animals that eat both animals and plants.

opaque   Blocks the passage of radiation; cannot be seen through.

oxygen–carbon dioxide cycle   The exchange of oxygen and carbon dioxide between plants and animals as a result of photosynthesis and respiration reactions.

passive solar heating   A method of heating with solar energy that does not require mechanical power to circulate the heat; instead, only natural conduction circulates the heat.

pendulum   A suspended weight that is free to swing back and forth.

periodic wave   See **wave.**

photon   A packet of energy that has both wave and particle properties.

photosynthesis   A chemical reaction in green plants in the presence of light in which carbon dioxide and water are changed to glucose (sugar) and oxygen; an endothermic reaction; an anabolic process.

pigment   A natural substance that gives color to a material.

pitch   A measure of how high or low a sound is.

polarized   A condition in which the positive and negative charges in a material are separated so that it has a positive and a negative end.

population   The grouping of organisms of the same species.

porous   Having holes.

positive terminal   A terminal with a positive charge.

potential difference   The difference in the volts between two terminals; a measure of the amount of push on electric charges; called **voltage.**

potential electric energy   Energy due to the attractive or repulsive forces between electrical charges.

potential energy   The stored energy of an object due to its position or condition.

pound   An English unit of force.

precipitation   The falling of water from the atmosphere in the form of rain, hail, snow, or sleet.

primary consumers   Animals that eat only plants; herbivores or omnivores; animals in the second trophic level.

producers   Organisms that can make their own food; autotrophs; plants; plants in the first trophic level.

product   A substance produced in a chemical reaction.

proton   A positively charged particle in the nucleus of an atom.

quarternary consumers   Organisms in the fifth trophic level; carnivores that eat any animal in lower trophic levels.

radiant energy   Energy traveling in the form of electromagnetic waves; radiation.

radiant heat   Heat transferred by radiation; infrared radiation.

radiation   Energy traveling in the form of electromagnetic waves; the method in which heat is transferred in the form of electromagnetic waves; the emission of infrared radiation.

radioactive decay   A nuclear reaction in which the nucleus of an unstable reactant spontaneously emits nuclear rays, forming a new element.

radioactive element   An element whose nucleus undergoes radioactive decay.

radio wave   A low-energy radiant energy used to carry signals to radios and televisions.

ramp A tilted surface used to move objects to a higher level; a type of machine.

rarefaction The region in longitudinal waves where the particles of the medium are pulled apart.

reactant A substance that is changed during a chemical reaction.

recycle To reuse.

reflect To bounce back from a surface.

renewable energy resource A natural resource that can be recycled, such as water and air, or replaced, such as plants and animals.

repel To push apart.

reproduce To produce new organisms like themselves.

repulsion Pushing apart.

reservoir rock Porous rock in which oil and natural gas collect.

resistance (R) The opposition of the flow of electric charges; measured in ohms.

resources All the natural materials and features of Earth that help support life and satisfy people's needs.

respiration The process by which plants and animals change food into energy and release carbon dioxide into the atmosphere.

revolve To move in a curved path around another object, such as Earth's motion around the Sun.

ripples Disturbances in a medium.

secondary consumers Animals that eat primary consumers; carnivores; animals in the third trophic level.

sediment Rock particle transported and deposited by water, wind, or glaciers.

solar energy Radiation from the Sun.

solar oven   A device that uses sunlight to cook food.

solution   A mixture of a substance that has been dissolved in a liquid.

sound   The brain's interpretation of sound energy.

sound energy   Mechanical energy transferred as a wave by vibrating particles.

sound wave   Longitudinal waves produced by sound energy.

space   The region beyond Earth's atmosphere; region with relatively no medium.

species   A group of organisms that are alike, such as roses or dogs.

spectral types   A category of stars that indicates their color and temperature.

spectroscope   An instrument used to separate light into colors.

speed of light   The speed that radiant energy travels; 186,000 miles (300 million meters) per second in a vacuum.

squared   In reference to an equation, the multiplication of a number by itself.

spontaneously   Happening by itself.

stable   Not likely to change.

standing wave   A wave that appears to remain still; a wave formed when two sets of waves with the same frequency and wavelength moving in opposite directions meet.

static charges   The buildup of stationary electric charges on an object.

static discharge   The loss of static electricity.

static electricity   A type of electricity due to the presence of static charges.

sterilization   A process that kills bacteria.

tanning   The process of turning the skin darker.

temperature   How hot or cold an object is; the measure of the average kinetic energy of the moving particles in a material.

terminals   The points at which connections are made to an electric device.

tertiary consumers   Organisms in the fourth tropic level; carnivores that eat secondary or primary consumers.

thermal conduction   The process of transferring heat through a conductor from one particle to another by collisions of the particles; this process is primarily due to the movement of free electrons in a conductor.

thermal conductor   A material through which heat is easily transferred.

thermal energy   The sum of all the energy of the particles making up an object; internal energy of an object.

thermal insulator   The name of an insulator when referring to its inability to conduct heat; a material that restricts the movement of heat.

thermal radiation   Radiation emitted by objects due to their temperature; ultraviolet radiation, visible light, infrared radiation.

thermometer   An instrument that measures temperature.

thunder   The loud sound produced by the expansion of air that has been heated by lightning.

top consumer   The top consumer in a food chain; the top level of an energy pyramid.

toxic   Poisonous.

transformed   Changed from one form into another.

translucent   Allows radiation to pass through but the radiation is spread in all directions.

transmutation   The change of one atom into another as a result of changes in the nucleus.

transparent   Allows radiation to pass through without changing its direction; so clear it can be seen through.

transverse wave   A wave in which the medium displacement is perpendicular to the motion of the wave.

trophic level   Each step in a food chain.

trough   Low part of a transverse wave.

ultimate consumer   See **top consumer.**

ultraviolet radiation (UV)   Invisible radiation that can burn the skin; its wave size is smaller than violet light.

universe   Earth and all natural objects in space regarded as a whole.

unmagnetized   Doesn't have an electric field; occurs when most of the domains in a magnetic material point in different directions.

unstable   Likely to change.

velocity   Speed in a particular direction.

vibration   Any motion that repeatedly follows the same path, such as a side-to-side or to-and-fro motion.

visible light   Radiation that the human eye can see; the small visible part of the electromagnetic spectrum.

visible spectrum   The different types of visible light arranged in order of wavelength. From highest to lowest wavelengths, they are red, orange, yellow, green, blue, indigo, and violet.

volt (V)   A unit used to measure the potential energy per charge in a battery.

voltage   See **potential difference.**

volume   The amount of space an object takes up.

water cycle   The continuous interchange of water between the ocean, the land, plants, and the atmosphere.

wave   A traveling disturbance that transfers energy, but not matter, from one place to another; also called **periodic waves**.

wavelength   Length of one wave.

weight   A measure of the force of gravity on an object.

wet cell   An electric cell with a liquid electrolyte, such as the cells in a car battery.

white light   A mixture of all the possible visible light waves.

wind   Air in motion.

windmill   A machine that converts wind into useful energy.

work (w)   The movement of an object by a force; the product of the force by the distance along which the force is applied. The process of transferring energy.

X-ray   Invisible radiation produced in nuclear reactions.

Index

Absorb, 59
Active solar heating, 178
Air, 29
Alloy, 142
Ampere (A), 134
Amplitude, 51
  longitudinal waves, 51
  transverse waves, 51,
    61–64
Antinodes, 59
Atmosphere, 29
Atom:
  definition of, 13
  energy levels, 73
  nuclear particles, 119
  nucleons, 119
  nucleus, 119
  parts of, 119–120
Attract, 119
Attraction, 19
Autotrophs, 175

Battery, 133–139
  definition of, 133
Bond, 13, 149
Burn, 151

Carnivores, 185
Celsius scale, 115

Charge. *See* electric charge
Charging by conduction,
  120
Charging by friction, 120
Chemical energy, 149–155
  definition of, 149
Chemical potential energy,
  149–155
  definition, 14, 29, 150
Chemical reaction:
  definition of, 13
  endothermic, 150, 153–154
  exothermic, 150
Chlorophyll, 151
Community:
  definition of, 185
  energy transfer through,
    185–194
Compound:
  definition of, 13
  ionic, 13
  molecular, 13
Compression, 51
Concentration, 127
Condensation, 171
Conduction, 90–95
  definition of, 90
Conductors:
  definition of, 92, 127